CAMBRIDGE LIBRARY COLLECTION

Books of enduring scholarly value

Music

The systematic academic study of music gave rise to works of description, analysis and criticism, by composers and performers, philosophers and anthropologists, historians and teachers, and by a new kind of scholar - the musicologist. This series makes available a range of significant works encompassing all aspects of the developing discipline.

Memoirs of Musick

Roger North (1651?–1734) was a successful lawyer and skilled amateur musician who became Attorney General to James II. After the 1688 Revolution he retired from public life and devoted his time to writing on a wide range of topics. *Memoirs of Musick* originally formed the final section of North's 1728 treatise on music theory, *The Musicall Grammarian*. It covers aspects of music history (or 'historico-critcall scrapps' as North calls them) from Ancient Greece to Corelli, and includes a substantial account of John Jenkins, who taught North the viol. Charles Burney quoted from the *Memoirs* in his *General History of Music* (1776–89), but this 1846 edition by the musicologist Edward Rimbault was the first time they appeared in print. The book includes an introduction on the manuscript of the *Memoirs* (now in Hereford Cathedral Library), a short biography of North and extensive explanatory notes to the text.

Cambridge University Press has long been a pioneer in the reissuing of out-of-print titles from its own backlist, producing digital reprints of books that are still sought after by scholars and students but could not be reprinted economically using traditional technology. The Cambridge Library Collection extends this activity to a wider range of books which are still of importance to researchers and professionals, either for the source material they contain, or as landmarks in the history of their academic discipline.

Drawing from the world-renowned collections in the Cambridge University Library, and guided by the advice of experts in each subject area, Cambridge University Press is using state-of-the-art scanning machines in its own Printing House to capture the content of each book selected for inclusion. The files are processed to give a consistently clear, crisp image, and the books finished to the high quality standard for which the Press is recognised around the world. The latest print-on-demand technology ensures that the books will remain available indefinitely, and that orders for single or multiple copies can quickly be supplied.

The Cambridge Library Collection will bring back to life books of enduring scholarly value (including out-of-copyright works originally issued by other publishers) across a wide range of disciplines in the humanities and social sciences and in science and technology.

Memoirs
of Musick

ROGER NORTH
EDITED BY EDWARD F. RIMBAULT

CAMBRIDGE UNIVERSITY PRESS

Cambridge, New York, Melbourne, Madrid, Cape Town, Singapore,
São Paolo, Delhi, Dubai, Tokyo

Published in the United States of America by Cambridge University Press, New York

www.cambridge.org
Information on this title: www.cambridge.org/9781108014830

© in this compilation Cambridge University Press 2010

This edition first published 1846
This digitally printed version 2010

ISBN 978-1-108-01483-0 Paperback

MEMOIRS OF MUSICK BY THE

HONOURABLE ROGER NORTH,

ATTORNEY-GENERAL TO JAMES II.

The Honourable
Roger North, Esq.
Ætatis cir 30.

MEMOIRS OF MUSICK

BY THE

HON. ROGER NORTH,

ATTORNEY-GENERAL TO JAMES II.

NOW FIRST PRINTED FROM THE ORIGINAL MS. AND
EDITED, WITH COPIOUS NOTES,

BY

EDWARD F. RIMBAULT, LL.D. F.S.A.

MEMBER OF THE ROYAL ACADEMY OF MUSIC IN STOCKHOLM ;

SECRETARY TO THE MUSICAL ANTIQUARIAN

SOCIETY OF LONDON, ETC. ETC.

" I verily think, and am not aſhamed to ſay, that, except Theology, no Art
is comparable to Muſick." *Martin Luther.*

LONDON:

GEORGE BELL, 186, FLEET STREET.

1846.

Preface.

THE " Memoires of Mufick," by the Honourable Roger North, were firft made known
to the world, through the extracts given
by Dr. Burney in the third volume of his
" General Hiftory of Mufic." The original
MS. was then in the poffeffion of the author's fon, the Rev.
Dr. North, Prebend of Windfor, the editor of his father's
works, the " Lives of the Norths," and the " Examen." At
the death of the Rev. Dr. North in 1779 the MS. in queftion,
together with feveral others, paffed into the hands of Roger
North, the author's grandfon, and from him to the Rev.
Henry North of Ringftead in Norfolk. At the fale of the
latter gentleman's library, about four years fince, the " Memoires of Mufick" had a very narrow efcape from deftruction, being purchafed, with a quantity of others, for a few
fhillings by one of thofe perfons who attend country fales
known by the defignation of brokers. The MS. however,

together with another, by the same author, entitled "A Discourse relative to the Bariscope," were fortunately seen and purchased by Mr. Robert Nelson of Lynn in Norfolk; and it is to this gentleman, in conjunction with Mr. G. Townshend Smith, Organist of Hereford Cathedral, to whom Mr. Nelson presented the MS. that we are mainly indebted for its appearance in the present form.

Mr. Smith, upon becoming possessed of the "Memoires of Musick" by the Honourable Roger North, lost no time in communicating the existence of the MS. to the Council of the Musical Antiquarian Society, and in the most liberal manner offered to place it at their disposal for publication. The Council, not feeling authorized, according to the formation of the Society, to commence a series of *literary* publications, suggested its independent publication to the present editor, and it accordingly appears under their sanction.

The MS. from which the "Memoires" are printed, is a small quarto volume of two hundred and sixty five pages, tolerably written, but in a somewhat strange and affected hand. The first portion of the volume consists of a treatise on the Science of Musick, entitled "The Musicall Grammarian," occupying one hundred and eighty-five pages. The remaining eighty form the subject of the present volume.

The work which the author modestly entitles "Memoires of Musick," as "not pretending to a compleat History," is an exceedingly lucid and well drawn sketch of the progress of the art, from the period of the ancient Greeks down to the commencement of the eighteenth century. It was written when the author was an old man, "quietly retired from the cares of office," and is the refult of a retentive memory, coupled with a knowledge and love of his fubject rarely met with among perfons in his ftation of life. As a fketch of the Hiftory of Mufic, and the various opinions concerning the art as they exifted in the writer's time, it may be confidered as comprifing not only the fruits of his own information and experience, but alfo of fome of the moft learned muficians of the day, the authority of whofe opinions is indeed frequently introduced. From the occafional careleffnefs and incorrectnefs of the ftyle, it is evident that the "Memoires" were never prepared by the author for the prefs; but in now prefenting it to the public it has been thought proper, with one or two very trifling exceptions, to adhere faithfully to the original MS.

The notes which have been added are the refult of much reading, and the peculiar facilities which the editor enjoys of confulting rare works. If their minutenefs be fometimes uncalled for in explanation of the text, the new and curious information they convey will, it is hoped, be fome excufe for their infertion.

E. F. R.

Grofvenor Cottage, Park Village Eaft,
Oct. 1, 1846.

Biographical Notice of the
Hon. Roger North.

HE Honourable Roger North was the fixth and youngeſt ſon of Dudley the ſecond Lord North. Of his family he has given ſome account in the preface to the Life of his brother the Lord Keeper Guildford; but of his own perſonal hiſtory little remains upon record, except what may be gleaned from the family memoirs of which he was the author.* He was born in the year 1650, and was originally deſigned by his father, who had " a

---

* *The Life of the Right Hon. Francis North Baron of Guildford, Lord Keeper of the Great Seal under K. Charles II. and K. James II.* 4to. Lond. 1742. With portrait of Lord Guildford by Vertue. (See the *Retroſpeƈtive Review*, ii. 238-56.)

The Life of the Hon. Sir Dudley North, Knt. and of the Hon. and Rev. Dr. John North. 4to. Lond. 1744. With portrait of Sir Dudley North by Vertue. (See the *Retroſpeƈtive Review*, v. 136-56.)

The Hon. Roger North's Life of the Lord Keeper is one of the moſt de-

fpecious fancy to have a fon* of each faculty or employ ufed in England," for the Civil Law. By the advice of his elder brother, Francis, his deftination was changed, and he was educated to the Common Law bar, in which branch of the profeffion it was in the power of his brother to render him fome very effential fervices. By his affiftance " a petit chamber, which coft his father fixty pounds," was procured for him, and to the fcanty allowance which fell to the fhare of a

lightful books of its kind in the world. Its charm does not confift in any marvellous incidents of Lord Guildford's life, or any peculiar intereft attaching to his character, but in the unequalled *naiveté* of the writer—in the fingular felicity with which he has thrown himfelf into his fubject—and in his vivid delineations of all the great lawyers of his time. In nice minutenefs of detail, and living picture of manners, it almoft equals the autobiographies of Benvenuto Cellini, Rouffeau, and Cibber.

* Of the fix fons of Dudley Lord North, the eldeft fucceeded to the title, and to the far greater part of no very large eftate. He appears always to have kept aloof from his brethren, who were left to ftruggle through the world, and rife to eminence by the force of their own attainments. The fecond fon Francis, afterwards Lord Keeper Guildford, led the way; and in him the others feem always to have found a fteady, able and affectionate friend, affiftant and advifer. For thefe reafons, and perhaps from the fuperiority of his talents, he was always ftyled their *beft* brother. The third fon Dudley, fought his fortunes abroad as a merchant. The fourth fon went to Cambridge, and rofe in the Church. The fifth fon Montague, was alfo a Levant merchant, and in partnerfhip with Dudley. The fixth and laft was Roger, the faithful friend and companion of his brothers, and the hiftorian of all their lives. We have faid *all*, for Montague North appears to have had little to diftinguifh him, and though no feparate memoir is written concerning him, that little is mentioned in different parts of the lives of his brothers. In the lives of the Norths we have an amiable fpectacle prefented to us of the youngeft of four brothers, remaining firmly and tenderly attached to each through life, and after their death fpending the laft years of his retirement from the world in recording their virtues and defcribing their actions.

younger brother, his affectionate relative made a timely addition. Nor was his kindnefs confined to pecuniary affiftance,
for while Roger North was yet a ftudent, the Lord Keeper,
who was then rapidly rifing into notice,* " caufed his clerk
to put into his hands all his draughts, fuch as he himfelf had
corrected, that by a perufal of them he might get fome light
into the formal fkill of conveyancing." The moft conftant
and affectionate intercourfe was maintained between the two
brothers, the Lord Keeper taking his younger brother with
him into all companies and entertainments, and always " pay-
ing his fcot." " I do not," fays Roger North, " remember
that he fo much as took the air without me, and fo when he
dined or fupped abroad, unlefs with grandees of one fort or
other, I was with him." When Francis was made Attorney
General, he divided the profits of one of the offices under
him with his younger brother; and when he became Treafurer of the Middle Temple, a perquifite chamber worth one
hundred and fifty pounds falling to his difpofal, he prefented
it to him in lieu of the fmall Student's Chamber, which he
had hitherto occupied.

Upon the promotion of Francis North to the feat of Chief
Juftice of the Common Pleas, he gave his brother " the coun-

---

* The Honourable Francis North was called to the bar on the 28th of June,
1661. In 1671 he was fworn into the office of Attorney General, and on the
fame day received the honour of Knighthood. In 1673 he was conftituted
Solicitor General, and in the following year Lord Chief Juftice of the Court of
Common Pleas. He was created a Peer of the realm, and appointed Lord
Keeper of the Great Seal on the death of the Earl of Nottingham in 1682.

tenance of practifing under him at *Nifi Prius*, and when he became a houfekeeper, Roger North and his fervant " were of his family at all meals."* On occafion of the fire which deftroyed a great portion of the Temple buildings, the Chief Juftice, who was unwearied in his kindnefs towards his brother, " fitted up a little room and ftudy in his chambers, in Serjeant's Inn, for the latter to manage his fmall affairs of law in, and lodged him in his houfe till the Temple was rebuilt, and he might fecurely lodge there. And his Lordfhip was pleafed with a back door in his own ftudy, by which he could go in and out to his brother to difcourfe of incidents; which way of life delighted his Lordfhip exceedingly." The practice of the younger brother appears to have advanced with the dignity of the elder. Upon the Great Seal being given to the latter, Roger North was made King's Counfel, and in the

---

* Roger North appears generally to have accompanied the Lord Chief Juftice in his circuits; and in one of thefe, at Exeter, " His Lordfhip agreeable to his great mafterfhip of Mufick, took notice of the Organ in the Cathedral Church, where the two fide columns, that carry the Tower, are lined with Organ-pipes, and are as columns themfelves. His Lordfhip defired the dimenfions of the great double diapafon; and the account as returned is thus,

	Feet.	Inches.
Speaking part, long	20	6
Nofe	4	0
Circumference	3	11
Diameter	1	3

Contents of the fpeaking part, 3 hogfheads, 8 gallons; weight, 360 pounds."

Life of the Lord Keeper, p. 119. The organ here noticed was built by John Loofemore in 1665. Lord Keeper North was " a mufician in perfection," and his biographer tells us that he has heard him fay, " that if he had not en-

three years enfuing acquired the better part of the fortune which he afterwards poffeffed. At this time he became a regular member of his brother's family, and had a coach and fervants affigned to him, " and all *at rack and manger*, for two hundred pounds a year, which was a trifle as the world went then." Of the tender intereft which the Lord Keeper took in the happinefs of his younger brother, a pleafing inftance is recorded by the latter. " Once he (Roger North) feemed more than ordinarily difpofed to penfivenefs, even to a degree of melancholy. His Lordfhip never left pumping till he found out the caufe of it: and that was a reflection what fhould become of him if he fhould loofe this good brother, and be left alone to himfelf, the thoughts of which he could fcarce bear ; for he had no opinion of his own ftrength to work his way through the world with tolerable fuccefs. Upon this

abled himfelf by thefe ftudies, and particularly his practice of Mufick upon his bafe or lyra viol (which he ufed to touch lute-fafhion upon his knees), to divert himfelf alone, he had never been a lawyer." (P. 15.) And again we are told that " his moft folemn entertainment was Mufick, in which he was not only mafter, but doctor," (p. 46,) and that " he was in town a noted hunter of Mufick-meetings." He publifhed *A Philofophical Effay of Mufick, directed to a Friend.* 4to. 1677: " Though fome of the philofophy of this Effay," fays Burney, (Hift. of Muf. iii. 475,) " has been fince found to be falfe, and the reft has been more clearly illuftrated and explained, yet confidering the fmall pro-grefs which had been made in fo obfcure and fubtle a fubject as the propagation of found when this book was written, the experiments and conjectures muft be allowed to have confiderable merit." Perhaps the moft perfect mathematical work on Mufic extant is a MS. in the hand-writing of Dr. Boyce, entitled " Harmonics, or an attempt to explain the Principles on which the Science of Mufic is founded." It was purchafed by Marmaduke Overend, Dr. Boyce's pupil, for fifty guineas, and is now in the Library of the Royal Inftitution.

his Lordfhip, to fet his brother's mind at eafe, fold him an annuity of two hundred pounds a year at an eafy rate, upon condition to repurchafe it at the fame rate when he was worth five thoufand pounds, and this was all done accordingly." The affectionate kindnefs thus difplayed towards him by his brother, made a proper impreffion upon the mind of Roger North, who entertained for his benefactor a tender refpect, amounting to veneration. During the reign of James the Second, who was very favourably difpofed towards the Lord Keeper and his family, Roger North was raifed to the poft of Attorney General; and about the fame time he was appointed Steward of the Courts under Archbifhop Sancroft.* The breaking out of the Revolution, and his well-known principles, foon however compelled him to retire entirely from public life. In 1690 he purchafed of Yelverton Peyton the Manor of Rougham in Norfolk,† and fpent large fums in enclofing and planting the lands, and in enlarging and improving the old hall.‡ He alfo built a library on the fouth

---

* Among the papers difcovered by Baker, after the Hon. Roger North's deceafe, was a curious autobiographical letter relative to his fervices in that capacity. It was partially communicated by Baker to Dr. Rawlinfon. (See Gutch's *Collectanae Curiofa*, vol. i. p. xxxvi.) Chalmers (*Biog. Dict.*) and Watt (*Bibl. Brit.*) are wrong in faying that he was Steward of the Courts to Archbifhop *Sheldon.* In the Harleian Collection, Britifh Mufeum, befides three volumes of letters written to Dr. Sancroft at different periods of his life, and from perfons of all defcriptions, are thirteen volumes (numbered 3786-3798) of mifcellaneous collections made by him, relating to a great variety of fubjects. Among them are preferved feveral of Roger North's official documents.

† See Blomefield's *Norfolk*, edit. 1809, vol x. p. 32.

‡ At the time when this manfion was occupied by Roger North, the net rent-roll of the whole eftate did not exceed 400*l.* per annum, fince which pe-

fide of the Church, and enriched it plentifully with books of his own and other benefactions.* His old age appears to have been chiefly paft " out of the way," as he expreffes himfelf, at this place where he died in the year 1733, at the age of eighty-three. He was married to Mary, the daughter of Sir Robert Gayer✝ of Stoke Pogis near Windfor, by whom he had two fons, Roger‡ and Montague,§ and five daughters, Elizabeth, Anne, Mary, Catherine, and Chriftian.

---

riod it has (through the fkill, induftry, and capital of the fucceeding tenantry) been gradually advancing, and is now let at no lefs a fum than 3540*l.* (*Gen. Hift. of Norfolk*, 1829, vol. ii. p. 831. *note.*) Among the improvements made in the old manfion by Roger North, was the addition of a mufic gallery fixty feet long, for which he had an organ built by Father Smith. Dr. Burney (*Rees' Cyclopedia*, article NORTH) fays, " There was not a metal pipe in this inftrument in 1752, yet its tone was as brilliant, and infinitely more fweet, than if the pipes had been all of metal." This organ is now in Dereham Church. (Vide *Gen. Hift. of Norfolk*, ii. 833.) Nothing now remains of the old hall at Rougham but fome of the foundation walls.

* See Blomefield's *Norfolk*, vol. x. p. 38. Among the books in the parochial library at Rougham was a choice collection of Eaftern Literature, collected by Dudleia the daughter of the fifth Lord North. " Thefe books to the difgrace of the parties concerned, were fold as wafte paper to a bookfeller, about forty years ago." (Vide *Gen. Hift. of Norfolk*, ii. 832.)

✝ See the author's preface to the *Life of the Lord Keeper*. Collins (*Peerage of Engl.* edit. Brydges, iv. 468) makes a fingular miftake in giving Roger North's wife and family to his brother Montague. Roger North, in the fame preface, where he fpeaks of *his* wife and family, exprefsly fays Montague " died without iffue." The writer of the Review of the *Lives of the Norths* (*Retrofp. Rev.* v. 130), fays that he " died *abroad;*" but Collins (iv. 468) tells us that he died 27th of Sept. 1710, and was buried at Rougham.

‡ The author of a *Difcourfe of the Poor, or the penurious tendency of the laws now in force.* 8vo. Lond. 1753. Nothing further is known of him.

§ Afterwards the Rev. Montague North, D.D. Prebend of Windfor, and the publifher of his father's works, the *Lives of the Norths* and the *Examen.* In

As a politician, it has been remarked, Roger North appears to have been honeſt, but deeply prejudiced in favour of thoſe high prerogative notions which were current after the Reſtoration, and which led him to defend ſome of the moſt corrupt meaſures of that period. Theſe principles led him to write an anſwer to Dr. White Kennett's *Complete Hiſtory of England*,* and occaſioned Horace Walpole to ſtyle him " the voluminous ſquabbler in defence of the moſt unjuſtifiable exceſſes of Charles the Second's adminiſtration."† His acquirements as a lawyer were probably conſiderable if we may judge from the high poſitions which he occupied, and from the profeſſional knowledge diſplayed in his *Diſcourſe on the Study of the Laws*.‡ The celebrated Earl of Clarendon

his dedication of the *Life of the Lord Keeper*, to the then Lord North, he ſays, " My father thought it his duty to leave behind him theſe papers, not only for the ſake of truth, but to make ſome return for the benefits heaped upon him by this illuſtrious anceſtor of your Lordſhip and his *beſt brother*." Dr. North was appointed Prebend of Windſor in 1775. He died 1779. See *Gentleman's Mag.* June 1775 (p. 304); Auguſt 1779 (p. 424).

   * *Examen; or, an Enquiry into the Credit and Veracity of a pretended Compleat Hiſtory of England*, 4to Lond. 1740. With Portrait of Roger North by Vertue. The original MS. is in Jeſus College, Cambridge. (See a critical examination of this work in the *Retroſpective Review*, vii. 183-217; viii. 1-30.) The *Examen* is valuable for the many original anecdotes it contains, and the view it preſents of party politics, but as an impartial authority it cannot be in any manner relied on.

   † Preface to the *Memoirs of King George II.—Poſtſcript*.

   ‡ *A Diſcourſe on the Study of the Laws, by the Hon. Roger North. Now firſt printed from the original MS. in the Hargrave Collection. With Notes and Illuſtrations by a Member of the Inner Temple*, 8vo. Lond. 1824. The editor in his Preface, which has been of great uſe to us in drawing up the preſent Memoir, ſays of this treatiſe, " As a guide to the ſtudy of the law as it exiſted

has left us his teftimony of Roger North's chara&er in the following paffage: "Jan. 18, 1688-9, I was at the Temple with Mr. Roger North and Sir Charles Porter, who are the only two honeft laweyers I have met with."* In the curious autobiographical letter refpe&ing his appointment as Steward of the Courts under Archbifhop Sancroft, the writer fays, "He [the Archbifhop] valued me for my fidelity, which, he being a moft fagacious judge of perfons, could not but difcern, and difpenfe with my other defe&s."† As a dilettante mufician he ranks defervedly high, and the beft proof of his talents is the found judgment and difcrimination by which he has been guided in drawing up the record of the progrefs of the art, as difplayed in the following pages.

in the writer's time, it may be confidered as comprifing not only the fruits of his own information and experience, but alfo of his brother the Lord Keeper Guildford, the authority of whofe opinions and pra&ice is indeed frequently introduced." It is fingular that of Roger North's various works only one was printed during the author's lifetime, i. e. *A Difcourfe of Fifh and Fifh Ponds*, printed in 1683. This book muft have been popular, for there was a fecond edition in 1713, a third in 1715, and a fourth in 1749.

* *Diary of the Earl of Clarendon from 1687 to 1690.* Printed in the Correfpondence, &c. 2 vols. 4to. 1828. Edited by S. W. Singer.

† *Colle&anea Curiofo.* Vol. i. p. xxxvi.

Memoires of Mufick

being

Some Hiftorico-Critticall Collections

of that Subject.

1728.

Advertisement.

HAVING dispatcht the Theory of Sounds, gramaticall speculations of Musick,* I doe not yet find in my selfe a full discharge of what I owe to that transcendant subject; but as a lover is not satisfyed in his rhapsodys to comend the beauty of his mistrefs, but he must needs search into her genealogie *cujus caput inter nubila*—so am I in mind urged to look as farr back into the family of our dear art, as my faint opticks will permitt; and the result here I have entitled Memoires, as not pretending to a full History, a work for Herculean shoulders, but onely to collect and modifye some Historico-criticall scrapps, hoping to be thereby eased of an incumbrance that as a dett lyes heavy upon my conscience.

---

* Alluding to *The Musical Grammarian*; the MS. treatise noticed in the Preface.

A Table of the Contents.

Memoires of Mufick.

N matters of antiquity there are two ex-
treams, 1. a totall neglect, and 2. perpetuall
gueffing; between which proper evidences
are the temper, that is, if there be any, to
make the beft of them—if none, to defift.
So hounds in a cold fcent are dilligent, and
all fcent failing, defift and hopelefsly trot away. This thought
came into my mind when I had a fancy to hunt after the
antiquitys of Mufick, and I had certainly acted the defpairing
hound, if fome perfonall memory and experience had not
detained me : for it hath fallen in my way to obferve, not
to fay practife, fome fpecies of mufick long fince antiquated,
and in that refpect may juftly be taken into the account of
antiquitys: and now being engaged in the recollection of
thofe, the inquifitive fpirit draws me back into the dark fpe-
culation of what mufick was in former ages, and if the refult in what follows fhall appear fond, erroneous, or frivo-
lous, in a pure effay, it may be excufed, the rather becaufe

neither religion, the ſtate, or good manners are like to be hurt by it.

We have large and ſubtile accounts of the muſick of the ancient greeks,* and after them the latins, with the addition of notes copious, and ſubtile commentations of moderne wrighters; and notwithſtanding all thoſe, wee are yet ignorant how (ſo much as in poſſibillity) to reconcile the miſterious modes, and effects reported of them: And many learned men have bin pleaſed to extoll the antique muſick as farr excelling the moderne, and the modernes no leſs learned, but as I take it, more ſkillfull, have pronounced the other to be

---

* The muſic of the ancient Greeks has engaged the attention of many ſearching antiquaries and patient mathematicians, and ſtill the ſubject is involved in conſiderable obſcurity—chiefly on account of the Greek term muſic being miſunderſtood. By moūſike (μουσική), the Greeks meant *poetry ſung*, with ſome ſort of accompaniment, and the moderns have fallen into error by overrating the importance of the melodic part, treating this as the principal, and poetry only as an ally. (Euclid, *Int. Harm.* p. i. edit. *Meibomius.*) It is thus we account for the effects ſaid to have been wrought by the effects of ancient muſic; for it is impoſſible that Plato ſhould have been thinking of mere vocal melody, and the ſounds of mean and imperfect inſtruments, when he ſaid (*De Legibus*, lib. ii.) that no change can be made in muſic without affecting the conſtitution of the ſtate, an opinion in which Ariſtotle acquieſced, and Cicero afterwards adopted: it is not to be credited that the laws of Lycurgus, ſet to meaſured ſounds by Terpander, were turned into a ſong, or that this Leſbian muſician quelled a ſedition in Sparta by ſinging ſome pretty air to the mob (Plutarch, *De Muſica*): it is abſurd to ſuppoſe that when Polybius tells us (lib. iv. 3) of a ſavage nation civilized by muſic, he means to ſay by coarſe pipes and guitars; and not leſs ridiculous is it to imagine that men were raiſed to the rank of chiefs and the dignity of legiſlators, ſolely on account of their taſte in ſinging, or their ſkill on the lyre or flute.

barbarous and unnaturall. This difference can never be reconciled, first becaufe, in matters of tafte there is no criterion
of better and worfe, and men determine upon fancy and prejudice, and not upon intrinfick worth. And next, becaus
wee have no fpecimens of antique mufick left for us (whereby as it were) to tafte the difference: and as for the fkill
and manner of performance, language is not fufficient to ex-
cite a juft idea of it. Therefore, caraçters apart, all wee
have to doe is to inquire by what means the ancients found
out and modeled the ufe of certain founds to gratifie the
fence of hearing, and thereupon inftituted the art called
Mufick. And then to obferve as well as wee may, the
changes that art hath undergone downe to our time. And
that I may not appear to faile overmuch in fo great an un-
dertaking, I muft aforehand declare that I pretend not to fee
further into the millftone then others have done, or may doe,
but propofe onely by conjecture, to enlighten fome obfcuritys,
whereof the reafons fhall be fhewed and fubmitted.

It is the misfortune of all arts, of which the ufe happens
to be difcontinued (leaving no reall fpecimens, which onely can
demonftrate what the practice of any fuch art was, except fome
dark verball defcriptions) and fo to fall into the catalogue of
the *artes deperditæ*, and be hardly, if ever recoverable. But yet
by fome cloudy expreffion found remaining, to make work
for crittiques, and the world litle the wifer; for arts have
peculiar termes, that is, a language underftood by the profeffors, and fome few elfe in the time; but in after times
when fuch arts are attempted to be revived, who fhould

3.
Ancient arts
knowne by
fpecimens
and not by
words.

make the Dictionary, or adapt things to the words ufed by obfolete authors. It is certain that nothing, but the very things appearing by fpecimens (if any are left) can doe it; and without fuch authoritys, become enigmatick. The mathematical arts have come downe to us intire, becaufe the fubject (quantum) is knowne to every body. Rhetorick and poetry bring their proper fpecimens with them, the old fpeeches and poems: Architecture but imperfectly, of which the antique is knowne almoft intirely by the veftiges yet actually, or in pictures, remaining; and without the help of fuch the formes of the ancient fabricks had never been gathered out of Vitruvius, who wrote on purpofe to inftruct them, and is not yet effectually underftood.

4.
Mufick def-
titute of prac-
tique exam-
ples. And this inconvenience hath happened to the fcience and practife of mufick in the higheft degree, for among the Greek republicks, that art was held in veneration, as if law, liberty, juftice, and morality depended upon it; and the modes and effects of it were the admiration, as well as delight of all men both wife and unwife: and according to the difpofition of the philofophers of thofe times, every naturall energye was moulded into a formall fcience. So Mufick had its fate; and from following nature, and imitation, was made an art with laws and rules not to be enumerated; as they fay the adding a ftring to an inftrument was made almoft high treafon.* And of this fubject we have authors upon

---

* This alludes to the ftory of Timotheus, one of the moft celebrated poet-muficians of antiquity, who, according to Paufanias (Lib. iii. cap. 12), added four new ftrings to the Lyre, or Cithara, in addition to the feven which it had

authors, and commentators upon them. But for want of reall or practicable specimens, it is not underftood what their mufick was, nor yet by meanes of all the pretended difcoverys, can any piece be accordingly framed, that mankind will endure to hear, although Kircher hath vainely attempted it.*

before. A curious *Senatus Confultum* againft him is preferved by Boethius (*De Mufica*, cap. i.) and thus englifhed by Stillingfleet (*Prin. and Power of Harm.* 1771, p. 136): "Whereas Timotheus, the Milefian, coming to our city, has deformed the ancient mufic; and laying afide the ufe of the feven-ftringed lyre, and introducing a multiplicity of notes, endeavours to corrupt the ears of our youth by means of thefe his novel and complicated conceits, which he calls chromatic; by him employed in the room of our eftablifhed, orderly, and fimple mufic, &c. It therefore feemeth good to us, the King and Ephori, after having cut off the fuperfluous ftrings of his lyre, and leaving only feven thereon, to banifh the faid Timotheus out of our dominions, that every one beholding the wholefome feverity of this city, may be deterred from bringing in amongft us any unbecoming cuftoms," &c. Athenæus (lib. xiv. with notes by Cafaubon, lib. viii. c. 11) fays, that when the public executioner was on the point of fulfilling the fentence by cutting off the new ftrings, Timotheus, perceiving a little ftatue in the fame place, with a lyre in its hand, of as many ftrings as that which had given the offence, and fhewing it to the judges, was acquitted. See alfo *Arati Phænomena*, ed. Oxon. 1672; Dr. Brown's *Differtation on Poetry and Mufic*, p. 128; Dr. Burney's *Hift. of Muf.* vol. i. p. 400; and Ed. Jones's *Lyric Airs*, preface, p. 7.

* Specimens of Ancient Greek mufic have been given by Vincenzio Galilei (*Dialogo della Mufica antica e moderna*, 1581); Hercules Bottrigari (*Il Melone, difcorfo armonico*, 1602); Kircher (*Mufurgia*, 1650); Edmund Chilmead (*Arati Phænomena*, Oxon. 1672); and M. Burette (*Hift. de l'Academie Royal des Infcript.* tome v.). An account of them may be found in Burney (*Hift. of Muf.* vol. i. p. 83, *et feq.*), where they are alfo given in modern notation with a conjectural rhythm. See alfo Böckh (*De Metris Pindari*, Lipf. 1811, iii. 12). Thefe fpecimens have been varioufly eftimated; probably the beft that can be faid of them is, that no certain notion can now be obtained of their real effect as anciently performed.

5.
Musick be-
gan with vo-
call pronun-
ciation.

I muft obferve that thefe affuming Greeks would needs have the originall, and invention of mufick, to have arifen amongft them. And for that end wee have poetick relations of dryed nerves in tortoife fhells,* fmith's hammers,† and

---

* A fingular ftory of the fuppofed invention of the Lyre is related by Apollodorus (*Biblioth.* lib. ii.). " The Nile," fays the Athenian mythologift, " after having overflowed the whole country of Egypt, when it returned within its natural bounds, left on the fhore a great number of animals of various kinds, and among the reft a tortoife, the flefh of which being dried and wafted by the fun, nothing remained within the fhell but nerves and cartilages, and thefe being braced and contracted by the drying heat became fonorous. Mercury walking along the banks of the river, happened to ftrike his foot againft this fhell, and was fo pleafed with the found produced, that the idea of a lyre prefented itfelf to his imagination. He, therefore, conftructed the inftrument in the form of a tortoife, [hence the name *teftudo*, Horace, *Od.* lib. iii. 11] and ftrung it with the dried finews of dead animals." The invention of the lyre is alfo attributed to Mercury by Paufanias (*Græc.* lib. viii. Arcad.), who ftates in addition, that Mercury found the tortoife-fhell on a mountain of Arcadia, called Chelydorea, near Mount Cyllene. The fame writer mentions a ftatue of Mercury, in the temple of Apollo at Argos, " holding a tortoife-fhell, of which he propofes to make a lyre." The Egyptian Guitar had only three ftrings; and it is to this inftrument Diodorus alludes (i. 16), when he applies that number to the lyre, which he fays correfponded to the three feafons of the year. Its invention he attributes to Hermes or Mercury, who taught men letters, aftronomy, and the rites of religion, and who gave the inftrument three tones, the firft to accord with fummer, the fecond with winter, and the third with fpring. That Diodorus confounds the guitar with the lyre is probable, from his attributing its origin to Mercury, who was always the fuppofed inventor of the latter; though there is reafon to believe that the fame fable was told him by the Egyptians in connection with the other three ftringed inftruments, and that it led to his miftake refpecting the lyre. " It was no doubt," fays Sir J. G. Wilkinfon, (*Manners and Cuftoms of the Ancient Egyptians*, ii. p. 298,) " from a conviction of the great talent required for the invention of an inftrument having only three chords [i. e. *ftrings*], and yet equalling the power of one with numerous

practitioners, as Apollo, Orpheus, &c. who might perhaps (as Homer) sing well to a petite instrument at feasts; But I am perswaded that, notwithstanding all these pretensions, Musick had an higher originall, and that is the use of voices, and language among men. And that having such facultys,

strings, that the Egyptians were induced to consider it worthy of the deity who was the patron of the arts ; and the fable of his intervention, on this and similar occasions, is merely an allegorical mode of expressing the intellectual gifts communicated from the Divinity, through his intermediate *agency*."

† We are told by Nicomachus, Gaudentius, Jamblichus, Macrobius, and all their commentators, that " Pythagoras, one day meditating on the want of some rule to guide the ear, analogous to what had been used to help the other senses, chanced to pass by a blacksmith's shop, and observing that the hammers, which were four in number, sounded very harmoniously, he had them weighed, and found them to be in the proportion of 6, 8, 9, and 12. Upon this he suspended four strings of equal length and thickness, &c. and fastened weights in the above-mentioned proportions, to each of them respectively, and found that they gave the same sounds that the hammers had done ; viz. the fourth, fifth, and octave, to the gravest tone ; which last interval did not make part of the musical system before, for the Greeks had gone no farther than the Heptachord, or seven strings, till that time." This is the substance of the account as abridged by Stillingfleet (*Principles and Power of Harmony*, p. 8). Upon examination and experiment it appears, that hammers of different size and weight will no more produce *different* tones on the same anvil, than bows or clappers of different sizes, will from the same string or bell. The effect also of their different weights fastened to strings was discovered by Galileo to be false. Bontempi, in trying the power of weights upon strings in the Pythagoric proportions of 6, 8, 9, 12, found, that instead of giving the fourth, fifth, and eighth, of the gravest tone, they produced only the minor third, major third, and tritonus ; so that the whole account falls to the ground. But though modern incredulity and experiment have robbed Pythagoras of the glory of discovering musical ratios by *accident*, he has been allowed the superior merit of arriving at them by meditation and design. Vide Aristid. Quint. (edit. *Meibomius*, p. 116) ; Montucla (*Hist. des Mathem.*) ; Euler (*Tentamen novæ Theor. Mus.*), and all other writers upon Harmonics and Temperament.

they muſt neceſſarily ſtumble upon the exerciſe of what wee call ſinging, that is, pronouncing with an open and extended voice; and however the flexures might be rude at firſt, in proceſs of time they would improve; eſpecially conſidering how uſefull ſinging was in the paſtoritiall life the primitive race of men led; among whom, any one having a clear and good voice, tho' purely naturall, muſt be a prime muſitian; and perhaps Tuball Cain, or Vulcan, might be ſuch a one, and merit the fame they have had for it.

6.
Nothing ex-
preſs before
K. David.

But to drop all theſe reflections, and come to the time of K. David, for before him all the notice of muſick wee have is of ſome ſongs in the Bible, of which nothing more is knowne, but that they were ſongs; and that ſhews, that in the higheſt antiquity there was vocall muſick. But when King David, for favour, invited good old Barzillia to his court, he excuſed himſelf (partly) by his being unable to hear the voices of ſinging men and ſinging women; which is a demonſtration that then there was an eſtabliſht muſick, and not onely vocall, as is there expreſſed, but inſtrumentall alſo* to attend them, as appears in the account of David's

---

* The conſtruction and uſe of muſical inſtruments have a very early place among the inventions attributed to the firſt inhabitants of the globe, by Moſes. No mention, however, is made in the Scriptures of the practice of muſic, till more than ſix hundred years after the deluge. But in Geneſis xxxi. and 26th and 27th verſes, about 1739 years before Chriſt, according to the Hebrew chronology, both vocal and inſtrumental muſic are ſpoken of as things in common uſe. The exact nature of the muſical inſtruments of the Hebrews is very uncertain. It is aſſerted in the Talmud that there were no leſs than thirty-ſix different ſorts; but this is againſt ſacred authority, which gives only ſixteen.

harping before Saul with his hand and fingers, and by the
Epigrafts to divers of the pfalmes, directed to the cheif mufitian,* and multitude of references to inftruments, and fome

---

However the monftrous fictions of the Talmudifts have deftroyed all confidence
in even their moft indifferent ftatements. Bafnage (*Hiſt. des Juifs*, lib. i. cap.
1) fays the Jews always "neglected the ftudy of arts and fciences; whereas the
Egyptians, under whofe bondage they groaned, had wit, learning, and ingenuity,
and pretended to an origin of much higher antiquity. Dr. Burney (*Hiſt. of
Muſ.* i. 255), fpeaking of ancient mufical inftruments, hazards the affertion
that "we have no account of any nation, except the Egyptians, where mufic
had been cultivated fo early as the days of David and Solomon; the Greeks at
that time having hardly invented their rudeft inftruments." Mufical hiftorians
have entirely overlooked the advanced ftate of mufic in Arabia. At a very
early period the Arabians poffeffed *thirty muſical inſtruments* (fee Foreign Quart.
Rev. No. 39, p. 108, where they are enumerated). There are feveral treatifes
extant upon mufic by Arabian writers, proving inconteftably that the art, and
even the fcience, was well underftood by this extraordinary people at a very
early period in the hiftory of the world. The work by Al Farabi (called the
Arabian Orpheus), treating on the principles of the Art or Elements of Mufic,
and the *Kitab ul Aguni*, a great Collection of Songs by Abulfaraji, A. D. 1226,
are in the Library of the Efcurial. The titles of many works of a fimilar
kind may be feen in the Index to the *Bibliotheca Arabica Hifpanica*, 2 vols.
folio, Madrid 1759.

In the firft book of Chronicles, chapters 15, 16, and 23, there is a particular
account and enumeration of all the muficians appointed by David in the fervice
of the ark, before a temple was erected. 1 Chron. xxiii. 5, David appoints
four thoufand of the Levites to praife the Lord with inftruments; and chap.
xxv. 1, the number of fuch as were *inſtructed* and were cunning in fong, is
faid to have been two hundred, fourfcore and eight. Before this time, it does
not appear from the facred writings, that any other inftruments than trumpets,
or finging, than in a general chorus of the whole people, was ufed in the daily
celebration of religious rites; though others are mentioned in proceffions, and
on occafions of joy and feftivity.

* The Hebrew word (למצת) rendered "chief-mufician," has not paffed
without difcuffion; but the general opinion which our tranflators followed

particularly with ten ſtrings* (which was not permitted to the Argives). And theſe muſitians were not of a precarious quallity as Homer, &c. to ſing to the kill-cows at feaſts,† but a royall conſort; and the king himſelf, who is ſtyled

---

ſeems to be well authorized. See Calmet's *Differtation ſur ces deux termes Hē-breux, Lămmātſeach et Sēla.* Aſaph, Heman, and Jeduthun were the three di-rectors of the muſic of the tabernacle, under David, and of the temple, under Solomon. Aſaph was *chief* maſter of muſic to David. (1 Chron. xvi. 7, and xxv. 6.) Aſaph had four ſons, Jeduthun ſix, and Heman fourteen. Theſe twenty-four Levites, ſons of the three great maſters of ſacred muſic, were at the head of twenty-four bands of muſicians, who ſerved the temple in turns. Their number there was always great, eſpecially at the grand ſolemnities. See Calmet's *Differtation.*

   * Pſ. xxxiii. 2; xcii 3; cxliv. 9. The inſtrument alluded to with *ten* ſtrings was probably the āſhūr. Some light might be thrown on the names of the various harps, lyres, and other muſical inſtruments of antiquity, if theſe mentioned in the Bible were more accurately defined; but much confuſion exiſts between the cithara or kitarus, the āſhūr, the ſambuc, the nabl, and the kinoor: nor can the various kinds of drums, cymbals, or wind inſtruments of the Jews be more ſatisfactorily aſcertained. The difficulty of identifying them is not ſurpriſing, when we obſerve how many names the Greeks had for their ſtringed inſtruments. See J. Pollux (iv. 9), and Athenæus (iv. cap. 25).

   † Muſic and dancing were conſidered eſſential at entertainments, among the Greeks, from the earlieſt times; and are pronounced by Homer (*Od.* i. 152) to be diverſions requiſite at a feaſt; "An opinion," ſays Plutarch (*de Muſica*), "confirmed by Ariſtoxenus, who obſerves that muſic is recommended in order to counteract the effect of inebriety; for as wine diſcompoſed the body and mind, ſo muſic has the power of ſoothing them, and of reſtoring their previous calmneſs and tranquillity." Such indeed, ſays Sir Gardiner Wilkinſon (*Mann. and Cuſt. of the Anc. Egyptians,* ii. 249), may have been the light in which the philoſophic mind of Plutarch regarded the introduction of theſe diverſions, and ſuch he attributed to the obſervation of the poet; but it may be queſtioned, whether they always tended to the ſobriety either of the Greeks or of the lively Egyptians.

Cytharardus, and (probably) the chief mufitian, precenter amongft them. And if wee may fuppofe the great men of thofe times to have bin fuch fcriblers as the Greeks were, and had works come downe to us, as theirs have done, what ftately accounts had wee had of the mufick of thofe times.

But now to trace a little the hiftory of mufick, we muft come again among the Greeks, who have left us books enough to fhow they had an art fo called, upon which their reftlefs witts and philofophers had refined infinite ways. But their accounts to us are *tantum non* hieroglifick. However, according to what I have obferved, and may guefs, that their ancient mufick (as that word implyes) lay chiefly in a continuity of verfes, which were fung to meafures, or fome long and fhort fyllables combined, which the poets call feet, without much variation or flexure, and that only as the accents require. So that a poem accented was without more adoe a fong; and that, pronounced in manner as fingers ufe, might be agreable mufick, even to us, efpecially if kept fteddy, as their ufe was, by an inftrument attendant. Much here might be tranfcribed out of Plutarch,* whofe difcours of Mufick

7.
Greek Mufick chiefly Song.

---

* Plutarch was not only a philofopher, mathematician, and hiftorian, but one of the moft diftinguifhed of the ancient theoretical muficians. His *Difcourfe on Mufic* contains more of the hiftory of ancient mufic and muficians than is to be met with elfewhere. It is written in dialogue, the fpeakers being Oneficrates, Soterichus, and Lyfias; the latter of whom at the requeft of Oneficrates gives a relation of the origin and progrefs of the harmonic fcience, down to the time at which he writes. Meibomius (Preface, *Antiq. Muficæ Auctores*), and Doni (*Præftantia Muficæ Veteris*, p. 65), are lavifh in their commendations of this treatife: the latter indeed calls it " a golden little work." A Latin

is both criticall and hiftoricall; but I can gather very little of diftinct notion out of it. It is faid there, that three things are neceffary to concur in good mufick, the found, the time, and the fyllable, all together at once, which is remarkable. And inftruments are fcarce ever mentioned but with refpect to poems. So that, fo farr as I can fee, a poet and a fidler were terms convertible and meant almoft the fame thing. But the changes afterwards happened to divide them, as will appear.

8.
Voices the originall of all Mufick.

During thefe elder times, which I may ftyle of the poets, and fo downe to thofe of the philofophers, in mufick the poem was the principall, and inftruments but occafionall, and for melioration, which regulated the tones of the fraile voice, for thofe of courfe would fall into accord with the inftrument; therefore the art of mufick was originated for the vocall exercife.

9.
Scales contrived from the manner of finging.

And the ordinary flexures of the voice in finging, however irregular and perhaps contingent at firft, gave occafion for the forming the feverall muficall fcales ufed by the ancients; for nothing els could adminifter to the fancy fuch *bizzarre*

---

text was printed at Venice in 1532, and a French tranflation appeared in 1610. Some doubts have exifted regarding its genuinenefs, but they have been fuccefsfully cleared up by M. Burette. (See *Mem. de l' Acad. des Infcript.* tome onzieme, Amft. 1736.) An Englifh tranflation may be found in Dr. Holland's edition of *Plutarch's Morals*, and alfo in the edition of the fame printed in 1684. In 1822, a new Englifh tranflation, accompanied with the original Greek text, was elegantly printed, for prefents only, by the Rev. J. H. Bromby, M. A. Vicar of Trinity Church, Hull.

gradations of founds as fome of them carryed ; and that is a proof of what was fayd, that finging was the firft muſick-maſter, and that neverthelefs fo becaus fome notes in the fcales are found juſt, for voices will naturally fall into a fort of tuneablenefs, which inſtruments might affiſt and make fteddy, fo that the voices might not fwerve as they are apt to doe ; but that the juft tune of muficall notes in fome fort or other is naturall may be obſerved by the finging of fome birds, and the common crys of the vulgar about the ſtreets ; but more efpecially when the fongs were reſtricted by num-bers poetically, for the returnes fell into the fame tones over and over againe. And it was obvious for the more curious to obferve the various tonations, and reduce them to a certain order, or fcale, which I fhall exhibit, and then it was prac-ticable to adjuft inſtruments fo as to humour and attend the voice in unifons : it is, as I fayd, rare to find any mention of muficall inſtruments without regard to voices, as if in practife they were for the moft part infeparable, and the poem equally allyed in both.

To make this genefis of the muſical art more familiar, I fhall ufe this image. We all know in what manner our ſtage players rehears their heroick verfes, with many too-high-too-low, in a pedantick manner, as fcoolmaſters ufe to whine out verfes of Virgill to their fcollars ; which is nei-ther finging nor fpeaking, but yet certain tones may be per-ceived in it. Now let an artiſt or philofopher come and obferve thofe tones, and he fhall difcerne the intervalls, and call them diefes, femitone, tone, or fourths, and accordingly

10.
Originall of
the Scales or
Tetrachords.

forme ſcales of notes, whereby Inſtruments may be contrived
to accompany in uniſons and choruſes, and together make a
pleaſing ſound, and by uſage grow formall in the manner,
and in the tones correct. One may gueſs that in theſe incep-
tives of muſick, there was not any variations obſerved exceeding a fourth; but within that ſpace divers orders of change.
And a fourth is a conſonance a voice is apt to fall into, and
there ſtopp; therefore in early times the cycle of all the
alterations was confined to that intervall, and then all to
returne by like ſtepps over again.   And this was the Tetrachord,* which regulated the tonations of the voice and inſtruments from the beginning of the muſicall art among the
Greeks, and continued but with more latitude for many ages,
even as I take it, to the time of Conſtantine, or lower downe
to the poſſeſſion of the Goths in Itally.

Of theſe Tetrachords there was three of different orders

---

* The fundamental ſyſtem in ancient muſic was the *tetrachord*, or ſyſtem of
four ſounds, of which the extremes were at an interval of a fourth. In modern muſic it is the octachord, and comprehends an octave between the extremes.   The important and peculiar property of the latter ſyſtem, namely the
completeneſs of its ſcale, was fully underſtood (ſee Ariſtides, p. 16, 17, edit.
Meibomius); but it was not taken in theory for the foundation of the ſcale, or
at any rate was conſidered as made up of two tetrachords.   Moſt of the modern writers, particularly Holden (*Eſſay towards a rational Syſtem of Muſic,*
Glaſg. 1770), have thought it neceſſary to conſider the octave as compoſed of
two fourths, which are disjoined or ſeparated by a tone.   As a practical introduction to muſical ſcience, remarks Dr. Callcott (*Muſ. Gram.* p. 21. edit.
1817), this arrangement may be conſidered as correct; although theory does
not allow the perfect mathematical equality of the fourths, in reſpect to the
places of the tones which compoſe them.

eftablifht, as I fhall fhew: And thefe were as laws among the Greeks, no other, or different order of notes, being ever fet up or pretended too in any of the cittys, or republicks; but in all other refpects they had peculiaritys of manner or time, which were nominally diftinguifht by countrys, as the Dorick, Phrigian, Lydian, &c.* And thefe manners were entertained and ufed in the feverall republicks as happened, or the governor thought moft proper, to incline the people to vertue and good order of living, and the philofophers recommended the fame accordingly. I waive the cure of Saul's frenzy by Mufick as miracular,† otherwife by what charme

---

* It is conjectured that there were originally only three modes, correfponding to the three fpecies of tetrachord, and that thefe were the Dorian, Phrygian, and Lydian. Thefe names derived from countries in Afia, afford ftrong proof that the mufical knowledge of the Greeks, and their fyftem, was derived from the Eaft. Afterwards this number of modes was increafed to feven, correfponding with the feven degrees of the octachord; they were denoted by the names Mixolydian, Lydian, Phrygian, Dorian, Hypolydian, Hypophrygian, and Hypodorian (Euclid, edit. *Meibomius*, p. 15). In the time of Ariftoxenus, the number of modes was thirteen and later writers reckon fifteen. (Euclid, p. 19. Ariftid. p. 23, 24.) The defcriptions of thefe modes are very fcanty, but they indicate pretty plainly that they were nothing more than tranfpofitions of the *greater perfect fyftem*. Particular meafures of poetry were confidered appropriate to different modes (Plat. *Legg.* ii. p. 670), and it has even been attempted to divide Pindar's Odes into Dorian, Æolian, and Lydian. (Böckh *de Metris Pindari*, iii. 15). See the chapter on the ancient Greek modes in Dr. Holder's *Treatife of the Natural Grounds and Principles of Harmony*, 1694, p. 133; and the learned article, Mufic, in Dr. Smith's *Dictionary of Greek and Roman Antiquities*. Lond. 1840.

† 1 Samuel, chap. xvi. This event happened, according to the Bible chronology, 1063 years before Chrift. Father Kircher has taken upon him to relate the whole progrefs of the difpofition of Saul by David; and has done it as

it was, wee cannot demonſtrate. But it is certain that amongſt the grecian republicks Muſick was idolized (as I ſayd), as if all religion, goverment, and good manners, depended upon it. And the ſtates intereſted themſelves to ſuſteine and incourage it, and to keep out innovations,* ſo that to add too, or alter the inſtruments, or modes, was almoſt piacular.

After all my wonder at theſe repreſentations, I can fix upon no reſolution but this, which is that the demon lay more in the poems then in the muſick; for it is plain how thoſe might operate upon mens moralls, but how mere modes of ſound ſhould doe more than make men merry or ſad is paſt all underſtanding. And there is ſcarce any account of Muſick, or of very little, which was had without poetry. And it is likely that the ſeverall modes ſo much ſpoke of for good or bad morall effects, referred to the ſubjects of the poems ſung with them, more then to the melody of the tunes. For if ſome modes were apt for idleneſs and levity, and others for ſolemnity and good living, the words were alwaies conformable, and being, as their manner was, diſtinctly and intelligibly pronounced, no wonder that the public authoritys in ſome places took notice of them. But beſides the uſing one or other of the Tetrachords, I preſume the cheif

---

circumſtantially as if he had been preſent at the time. (See *Muſurgia Univer-ſalis*, Rome, 1650. tom. ii. p. 214, et ſeq.)

 * "It was not allowable for painters, or other imitative artiſts, to innovate or invent any forms different from what were eſtabliſhed ; nor lawful, either in painting, ſtatuary, or any branches of muſic, to make any alteration." (Plato, *De Legibus*, lib. ii.)

differences of thefe modes confifted in the manner of the parts or time. As if inftead of German, Itallian, or French modes, wee fhould fay Andante, Allegro, or Current and the like. Wee ufe all modes promifcoufly but the Greeks affected the modes of their peculiar country, and feldome any other. It is not ftrange that neighbouring people fhould have different ufages efpecially in their mufick, which was their wonder, care, and delight, and a fubject of their philofophers fubtilery. But wherein confifted the manner of their practife, fo intirely in ufe and with effects difcrepant from ours, I think, cannot be made appear, tho' many of our witts & critiques have fweat about it.

But wee muft alfo confider, that the people varyed their modes more or lefs in the confequence of time; for notions as well as practife are alwaies in a way of alteration, efpecially among the Greeks, that fwarmed with witts and philofophers, who were alwaies at work inventing fome new thing; their ordinary poetry and heroicks diverfifyed, as the fingers contrived clufters of longum and breve fyllables, called feet. In the firft vol. of St. Auftin's works* there is an

13.
Mufick fubject to continuall change.

* St. Auftin, or Auguftine, was born in Africa, A.C. 354, and died 430. Befides the fix books written by him upon Mufic, which are printed in the folio edition of his works at Lyons 1586, there is a MS. tract of his writing in the Bodleian Library, entitled *De Mufica*; but it is nothing more than a fermon in praife of Church Mufic, nor do his fix books contain any other rules than thofe of Metre and Rhythm. Two ancient MSS. of the fourteenth and fifteenth centuries, of the fix books on Mufic may be feen in Britifh Mufeum, Royal MSS. II. E. xi. and Harl. MSS. 5248.

operofe tract of Mufick, but more properly of poetry, for it is almoft wholly upon feet, of which there is a catalogue enough to fright a minor poet; a mere profodia or any thing rather then mufick, of which there is not the leaft difcovery. But admitting that changes, or as they accounted them improvements (and thefe moftly of inftruments) advanced; yet the principles of their mufick, by which the poetry and voices were regulated, that is the feverall fcales of tones, or Tetrachords, continued the fame downe thro' the empire even to the Gothick times. And however the inftruments varied in compafs, yet they conformed to the modes of the voices, and were for the moft part attendant upon them, feldom acting apart; but after Tetrachords and diapafons were heaped one upon another, beyond the compafs of fong, inftruments broke loofe and often acted feverally, as in the ftory of Themiftocles and other paffages in antiquity.* But as to the grand revolution of muficall affaires I fhall have them in confideration when I have done with the Tetrachords.

---

* Cicero obferves (*Tufc. Quæft.* lib. i.) that " they (the Greeks) confidered the arts of finging and playing upon mufical inftruments a very principal part of learning; whence it is related of Epaminondas, who, in my judgment, was the firft of all the Greeks, that he played very well upon the flute. And, fome time before, Themiftocles, upon refufing the harp at an entertainment, paffed for an uninftructed and ill bred perfon. Hence Greece became celebrated for fkilful muficians; and as all perfons there learned mufic, thofe who attained to no proficiency in it were thought uneducated and unaccomplifhed." Cornelius Nepos, again, mentioning Epaminondas, obferves that " he played the harp and flute, and perfectly underftood the art of dancing, with other liberal fciences; though," he adds, " in the opinion of the Romans, thefe are trivial things, and not worthy of notice, yet in Greece they were reckoned highly commendable."

The Tetrachords or fcales of muficall tones were three, which *ec nomine* declares a fundamentall error, for in the truth of things, which we call nature, there can be but one, as later experiments have demonftrated, of which in proper time. One of thefe fcales was called the Diatonick, and for degrees hath a femitone, and two tones to come at the fourth. This agrees well with the Orphean harp,* and finally hath got the better of all the reft, and (with fome improvement, as being moft aggreable to nature) reigns in the moderne muficke at this day. The next is the Chromatick, which ftepps by two femitones, and a tritemitone, or flat third into the fourth. And from hence our mafters call all movement by femitones, Chromatick. The other fcale is called the En-harmonick ; which by its name one would expect had moft of harmony, but in truth there is litle or none belongs to it ; for the fteps are by two diefes or (as wee terme them) quarter notes, and then into the fourth by a ditone, or third fharp.

---

* The firft Mercurian harp, or more properly lyre, had at moft, but four ftrings. Others were afterwards added to it by the fecond Mercury, or by Amphion ; but according to feveral traditions preferved by Greek hiftorians, it was Orpheus who completed the fecond tetrachord, which extended the fcale to a heptachord, or feven founds. The affertion of many writers that Orpheus added two new ftrings to the lyre, which before had feven, clafhes with the claims of Pythagoras to the invention of the octachord, or addition of an eighth found to the heptachord, which made the fcale confift of two disjunct inftead of two conjunct tetrachords, and of which almoft all antiquity allows him to have been the inventor. Nor is it eafy to fuppofe that the lyre fhould have been reprefented in ancient fculpture with four or five ftrings only, if it had nine fo early as the time of Orpheus, who flourifhed long before fculpture was known in Greece.

And thefe two laft feem to differ cheifly as a flat third and a fharp third. And that the comings to them, were but as graces, and the emfafis refting upon the fourth ; for to begin with a femitone or lefs, when mufick requires a tone to be the fecond found, muft be difcordant upon any other account.* And the Ditonean fcale as they ufed it is not without this fault, unlefs it is ufed as the common beat upon rifing into a found from the femitone below which the mufitians ufe at the entrance of their play.

15.
Enharmo-
nicks Imprac-
ticable.

It is difficult to tune thefe fcales, and the Enharmonick feems out of the power of ears to adjuft ; for who can hear

---

* In order to make the honourable writer's explanation of the ancient *Greek genera* perfectly clear, it will be neceffary to exemplify it in mufical notation. The Greek muficians (as we have feen) ufed three genera : I. THE DIATONIC, in which the intervals between the four founds were (afcending) femitone, tone, tone :— II. THE CHROMATIC ; femitone, femitone, tone and half :— III. THE ENHARMONIC ; diefis, diefis, double tone :— (The fecond note is made to reprefent a found half way between E and F, for which the modern fyftem fupplies no notation.) Of thefe genera the diatonic was allowed to be the moft ancient and natural, and the enharmonic the moft modern and difficult ; the latter, however feems to have become the favourite with theorifts at leaft, for Ariftoxenus complains that all writers before his time had devoted their treatifes almoft entirely to it, to the neglect of the two others (Ariftoxenus, p. 2 and 9, edit. *Meibomius*). See alfo the excellent and elaborate paper on Greek Mufic in Dr. Smith's *Dictionary of Greek and Roman Antiquities*.

when the diefis' are right? And fuppofing them juft, they can have no confonance with any other, for take any interval that is muficall, and add, or detract a diefis, and it becomes damnable difcord. It is faid of Pythagoras (Plut. *Archuf. Irlandro Interprete*) that he difallowed the making a judgment of mufick by the fenfes,* but he would have it approved by the fubtilety of the mind, and harmonicall proportion, and

---

* Pythagoras paid the greateft attention to the fcience of Mufic, and confidered one of the nobleft purpofes to which it could be applied was to foothe and calm the mind (Plutarch *de Virtute morali.* Strabo, lib. i. p. 11, *ed Cafaubon.* Jamblich. *de Vita Pythag.* &c.). He deemed it the duty of a philofopher to look upon it as an intellectual ftudy, rather than an amufement, for his gravity cenfured the cuftom of judging Mufic by the fenfes, and required that it fhould be fubmitted to the acumen of the mind, and examined by the rules of harmonic proportion (Plutarch *de Mufica*). It was the idea of this philofopher " that the air was the vehicle of found, and that the agitation of that element, occafioned by a fimilar action in the parts of the founding body, was its caufe. The vibrations of a ftring, or other fonorous body, being communicated to the air, affected the auditory nerves with the fenfation of found; and this found," he argued, " was acute or grave in proportion as the vibrations were quick or flow." Others were of a different opinion; and Ariftoxenus held the ear to be the fole ftandard of mufical proportions. He efteemed that fenfe fufficiently accurate for mufical, though not for mathematical purpofes; and it was, in his opinion, abfurd to aim at an artificial accuracy in gratifying the ear, beyond its own power of diftinction. He therefore rejected the velocities, vibrations, and proportions of Pythagoras, as foreign to the fubject, in fo far as they fubftituted abftract caufes in the room of experience, and made Mufic the object of intellect, rather than of fenfe. Modern inveftigations, however, have confirmed the ftatements of Pythagoras, and abfolute demonftration has placed them beyond the poffibility of doubt. Jamblichus informs us that Pythagoras derived his information upon different fciences from Egypt, and taught them to his difciples (Jambl. *de Vita Pythag.* lib. i. c. 29); that he learnt philofophy from the Egyptian priefts (*Jambl.* i. c. 28); and that he employed Mufic for curing difeafes both of body and mind (*Jambl.* i. cc. 25, 29, and 31).

not by the faculty of hearing. *O Mirum !* And there it is complained that of late the majesty of the ancient diatonicks are slighted, and many grow so dull, to account the enharmonick diefes infenfible, and out of an habitude of mind account what they doe not perceive as next to nothing, and unprofitable, with more of such unintelligible geare, as would fooner burst, then edifye a mans understanding, that should go about to unridle it.   But as I have pickt out a litle here, so another may fqueze out some further mifty conjectures, and so, with labour in vain, tire upon the subject till doomsday.

16.
Chromatiq.
little better.

The Chromatick hath not much advantage in practis, for it steps by two femitones, and then leaps over a flat third into the fourth, which is an inscrutable miftery, and inconfiftent with melody, and (as the other) not to be reconciled, but by following an humour in finging verfes, which one may imagine to play to and fro, falling or rifing, with the voice by fmall intervalls, and fometimes letting it vary a third or a fourth, that is bringing irregular ufages, as the variegated founds of finging birds, into an artfull difcipline; and as for the Diatonick I fhall fay no more here, but that it referrs alfo to finging, and by help of inftruments growing upon it, it become at length Guidonian.

17.
Greeks continually difpofed to change.

These fcales were extended by fetting one over another, and the fecond tetrachord came up within a tone of the diapafon.   But another like tetrachord following did not anfwer by diapafons to the first; therefore a stop was made there, and to fullfill the diapafon, a note was added below out of all

tetrachord, which was called *Proflambanomenos;* as if two tetra-chords reached from G to F then F F was the gained note. And thus the compafs of a full diapafon was gained, which Pythagoras fayd was enough for the purpofe of mufick.* Wee muft needs fuppofe that a bufy fubtile people given to arts and fciences, and all emolous of one & other, as the Greek republicks were, would never let their favourite arts of poetry and mufick be ftagnant in any manner, without perpetuall profers of alteration, and fome fucceeding, by many thought for the worfe (as from the majefty of the ancients, or from the ditones to the chromes and harmonicks) and with fome,

---

* " It is not to be fuppofed," remarks the learned writer of the article Greek Mufic in Dr. Smith's *Dictionary of Greek and Roman Antiquities,* " that the tetrachord could long continue to furnifh the entire fcale ufed in practice, though it was always confidered as the element of the more comprehenfive fyftems which gradually came into ufe." The theory of the genera, as has been feen, required only the tetrachord for its full development, though it certainly could not have been invented till after the enlargement of the fcale. When two tetrachords were joined fo that the higheft found of one ferved alfo for the loweft of the other, they were faid to be *conjunct.* But if the higheft found of one were a tone lower than the loweft of the other, they were called *disjunct,* thus B C D E F G A—*conjunct;* E F G A B C D E—*disjunct.* A hendè-cachordal fyftem, confifting of three tetrachords, of which the middle one was conjunct with the lower but disjunct from the upper, thus, B C D E F G A-B C D E is fuppofed to have been ufed about the time of Pericles (See Böckh, *de Metris Pindari,* lib. iii.). Afterwards a fingle found called *Proflambanomenos* was added at an interval of a tone below the loweft found, and a conjunct tetrachord was added above. And thus arofe a fyftem of two complete octaves, which was called the *greater perfect fyftem.* Another fyftem, called the *fmaller perfect fyftem,* was compofed of three conjunct tetrachords, and thefe two toge-ther conftituted the *immutable fyftem,* defcribed by all the writers later than Ariftoxenus, and probably known to him. (See Euclid, p. 17, edit. *Meibomius.*)

novelty of modes and verfifying, but continually to vary, and
that moftly by inlarging its territorys; and accordingly tetrachords were pyled up, and the notes honoured with diftinct
appellations, with marks to each which fet over the fyllables
of verfes inftructed the mufick, and the rations of the intervals fubtilized, and the rationale of harmony drawn out of
numbers, deferring little to the fence of hearing, which it
feems without mathematicks could not diftinguifh between
right and wrong; and all with infinite refining, which is a
demonftration that they were upon a wrong bottom, and
worked upon falfe principles; for as well in matters of arts
and action, as in difcours; trifling, verbofity, and cobling,
are never fo copious and redundant, as when principles are
falfe, whence proceeds all manner of obfcurity and confufion,
both in notion and expreffion.

18.
Of the tibia
and fiftula.

It is a large branch of this fubject, to gaine fome cogni-
zance of inftruments—thefe were either flabile or nervous;
the former were either trumpets* (*tuba*), tibia,† or fiftula,

---

* The *Tuba* or long trumpet, called by the Hebrews the Trumpet of the
Jubilee, may be feen in feveral pieces of ancient fculpture at Rome, particularly
on the Arch of Titus, and on Trajan's Pillar. Burney (*Hift. of Mufic*, vol. i.
pl. 4.) has given a reprefentation of the ancient *Tuba* from a *Baffo relievo* at
the Capitol, reprefenting the triumph of Marcus Aurelius. The trumpet does
not appear to have been in very early ufe among the Greeks, and it is rarely
mentioned by Homer at the fiege of Troy, where the chief inftruments were
the flute, lyre and pipe. The trumpet was however known in Greece before
that event. Athenæus (iv. 25) fays it was the invention of Minerva, or of
Tyrrhenus, a fon of Hercules. The Greeks according to Wilkinfon (*Manners
and Cuftoms of the Ancient Egyptians*, vol. ii. p. 263) had fix fpecies of trum-

and the other divers forts of harps.‡ The trumpets were ufed in warr, as the roman litua, but were not drawne into any tetrachord nor joyned with voices. The tibia, or fiftula

---

pets; the Romans four, in their army—the *tuba, cornuus, buccina,* and *lituus.* They were the *only* inftruments employed by them for military purpofes, and in this they differed from the Greeks and Egyptians.

† The *Tibia* was originally a flute made of the fhank, or fhin bone of an animal; and it feems as if the wind inftruments of the ancients had been long made of fuch materials as nature had hollowed, before the art of *boring* flutes was difcovered. The *Fiftula* was compofed of a number of reeds, of different lengths, tied together. It was alfo known as the *Syrinx.* This fimple inftrument preceded the invention of *Foramina,* or holes, by which different founds could be produced from the fame pipe. (Virg. *Buc.* ii. 32, 36.)

‡ The Harp is an inftrument of very high antiquity, and was in conftant ufe among the ancient Egyptians. They varied greatly in form, fize, and the number of their ftrings; and are reprefented in the ancient paintings with four, fix, feven, eight, nine, ten, eleven, twelve, fourteen, feventeen, twenty, twenty-one, and twenty-two ftrings. They were frequently very large, even exceeding the height of a man, taftefully painted with the lotus and other flowers, or with fancy devices; and thofe of the royal minftrels, in the tombs of the Kings at Thebes, were fitted up in the moft fplendid manner, adorned with the head or buft of the monarch himfelf. The oldeft harps found in the fculptures are in a tomb, near the pyramids of Geezeh, between three and four thoufand years old. They are more rude in fhape than thofe ufually reprefented; and though it is impoffible to afcertain the precife number of their ftrings, they do not appear to have exceeded feven or eight, and are faftened in a different manner from ordinary Egyptian harps. See Sir J. G. Wilkinfon's *Manners and Cuftoms of the Ancient Egyptians,* vol. ii. p. 222, *et feq.* The Harp does not appear to have been known to the ancient Greeks, but many ftringed inftruments, as the Cithara, went from Afia to Greece: and this laft, according to Plutarch, (*de Mufica*) was originally ftyled Afiatic. The fame author obferves that the cithara was employed upon facred and feftive occafions, and Heraclides, of Lefbos, fuppofed it to have been invented by Amphion; but a diverfity of opinion always exifted upon the fubject of its introduction into Greece. By the Harp, then, we are to underftand that the honourable writer means the

were allwaies muficall. It is faid the tibia had four foramina,* which I fuppofed anfwered fome tetrachord, and in
fonoroufnefs imitated the trumpet, by which I guefs it was
voiced either by the lipps, as a cornett, or els by fome reedall.
How the fiftula was voiced I can fcarce guefs; if it had bin
after the flute manner, like our comon organ pipes, fome
difcription would have fhewed it, but the unhappynefs is
fuch, that out of all the philophicks, and fculptures of anti-

---

Lyre or the Cithara, which in the times of the early Greeks and Romans were
the fame inftrument. (See *Paufan. Græc.* lib. iii.) In later times the Cithara
refembled the modern guitar.

* The flute was at firft very fimple, and as Horace obferves, "with a few
holes;" the number being limited to four, until Diodorus of Thebes in Bœotia,
added others; improving the inftrument at the fame time, by making a lateral
opening for the mouth. See Jul. Pollux (*Onom.* iv. 10). Clonas, who lived
many years after Terpander, was faid to have been the firft to invent laws and
fuitable airs for the flute, though thefe were fuppofed to have been borrowed
from the Myfians. (See Plutarch, *de Muficā*.) The ancient flutes were made
of reeds, box-wood, laurel, metal, filver, and even gold; and of fuch value
were fome of thefe inftruments, that Ifmenias, a famous Theban flute-player,
is faid to have paid three talents (nearly 600*l.* fterling) for a flute. Ifaac Voffius,
fpeaking of the ancient flute (*De Poematum Cantio et Viribus Rythmi*, Oxon.
1673), fays, "How great the care and diligence of the ancients were in improving this inftrument, fufficiently appears from what both Theophraftus and
Pliny have wrote concerning the reeds of the lake Orchomenius. It was not
fufficient that they were cut at certain periods of years, when the lake was
become dry; unlefs they were alfo macerated by the fun, rain, and froft, and
afterwards foftened by long ufe; and remaining without any defect fatisfied the
wifh of the artifts. He who reads thefe things will the lefs wonder that
fometimes *tibia* have been fold for feven talents, as Lucian teftifies." The
various forms of the early flute are depicted in Merfennus (*De Inftrumentis
harmonicis*, forming the fecond part of the *Harmonicorum*, Paris, 1636); and
in Blanchinus (*De tribus generibus Inftrumentorum Muficæ veterum Organicæ
Differtatio*, Rome, 1742).

quity, there is no glimpfe of any device whereby thefe pipes were made to found,* tho' it had bin a fubject for Pythagoras to have obferved as worthy as to note the tones of a fmith's anvill.† But it is certain they had no great compafs, and that not very juft, it not being eafy to give pipes and the foramina juft accord on unifon tones. And there is reafon to think the double mouthed or fpread tibia ufed at facrifices were unifons and had no foramina; for in the columnes the piping boy is made to hold his hands upon the two tibia's full gripe without any figne of foramina or fingering, which one would think fhould, as well as greater nicetys, have bin expreffed if any fuch had bin in ufe.‡ But at Baccanall feafts and weddings the antiq. *bafreleivs* fhow double pipes, and (by the pofture of the fingers) foramina;§ but which were tibia, and which fiftula, for the forms are various, is hard to fay   But it feems very certain that in the Theatres onely the tibia were ufed and not harps.

---

* The pipes of the *fiftula panis*, being compofed of reeds or canes cut juft below the joint, were all *ftopt pipes*, like thofe in the ftopt diapafon of the organ, in which the wind is emitted at the fame place where it enters; and as it has a double motion to make, twice the length of the tube, the tone is an octave lower of a *ftopt pipe*, than of an open one of the fame length and diameter.

† See note ante.

‡. Double flutes of equal length and diameter, without holes or ftopples, are frequently depicted on ancient vafes and fculpture. See Sir W. Hamilton's *Etrufcan Antiq.* vol. i. pl. 124. The found produced muft have been of the trumpet kind.

§ See the two beautiful paintings, which were found at Refina and Cività Vecchia, and which reprefent Marfyas teaching the young Olympus to play on the double pipe. (*Ant. d' Ercolano*, i. tav. 9; iii. tav. 19.)

The mention of theatres put me in mind to obferve divers things to confirme what hath bin fayd concerning mufick following the manners of the voice. It is fayd that Gracchus an impetous orator, had a piper ftood behind him to quallifie the tones of his fpeeches to the people,* which the ftraining to be loud had turned to a right downe finging, with acutes and graves, fo as a pipe might conforme, which cannot be done to our ordinary fpeaking or preaching. And this was (nearly) the fame as *tibias canere,* and feems to unridle the wonderfull ufe of the tibia in theatres of which I fhall take notice afterwards. A man might be Cytharedus and fing to his owne harp; and whilft that inftrument was ufed, the poet and the mufitian might be (and for the moft part was) the fame. But when the fong was to be attended by wind inftruments, the poet and the mufitian or finger divided; for one could not performe both. It is fayd by Plutarch,†

* Orators, though not conftantly accompanied by an inftrument, had their voices fometimes regulated by one. That generally employed was a fort of pitch-pipe, called a *tonorium.* Both Cicero (*De Orat.* lib. iii.) and Plutarch (*Vit. C. Gracch.*) relate the well known ftory of the voice of the furious tribune, Caius Gracchus, being brought down to its natural pitch, after he had loft it in a tranfport of paffion, by means of a fervant placed behind him with a *tonorium.*

† "It was a cuftom among the ancients, and continued down to the period when Melanippides wrote his dithyrambics, for performers on the flute to engage their fervices for hire to the poets and compofers of mufic, their province being held in higher efteem than that of the flute-players, who were confidered in the light of fervants to the compofers, and bound to conform fcrupuloufly to their inftructions. But in procefs of time this fubordination ceafed; and the confequences are defcribed in a lively manner by the comic poet Pherecrates,

that the poets were fain to hire the wind mufick and pay
'em; which was an excife upon witt, unlefs it were in order

who introduces Mufic on the fcene, in the perfon of a female, covered from
head to foot with wounds. He reprefents her as interrogated by Juftice,
perfonated alfo by a female, on the caufe of her miferable ftate, and anfwering
thus:

MUSIC.

Gladly will I explain: the pleafure mine
To tell my forrows, if to liften thine.
The guilty origin of all my wrongs
Is Melanippides. To him belongs
The dire defign alas! by victory crowned
My ftrength to diffipate. On twelve cords bound
He torturing held me; and beneath his fway,
Relaxed and faint, my powers diffolved away.
Yet not to Melanippides alone
I owe the evils under which I groan;
For curfed Cinefias, of Athenian race—
O! may his name be covered with difgrace!
Varying with modulation wild each ftrain
And fpurning Harmony's allowed domain,
Bereaved me of whatever grace was mine.
Juft like the fhield, the dithyrambic line
The form reverfes which it gives to view,
Nor is to order and to nature true.
Yet will not thefe harfh foes fo harfh appear,
When all my other injuries you hear.
For Phyrnis, with the fury of a ftorm
And eddying whirlpool, twifted all my form;
And by a mifchievous contrivance wrings
Twelve harmonies from my five fimple ftrings.
Yet though from him fo many wrongs I date,
I can forgive his temporary hate:
For though he erred, he penitent confeffed
His errors, and my grievances redreffed.
But deareft Lady! would you truly know

to ſerve publick celebration as in the theatres.   For ſongs to the harp and to the fiſtula as I gueſs were proper for chamber muſick, that required a tranquillity to be familliarly heard.

It is probable that after the harps were devided from the ſimplicity of a few ſtrings, and new forms were deviſed, and many ſtrings added, the handling became a peculiar art, and the performers were (as in latter times) proud of their play, and uſing their inſtruments perhaps ſingly and without voices, they ſhewed divers harmonious tricks upon them as wee doe now adays upon ours ;* but as for that which wee call con-

---

From whom my deepeſt wounds and miſeries flow,
It was Timotheus drove me from the earth.
JUSTICE.
Say who is he ? What country gave him birth ?
MUSIC.
Miletus ; and he owns another name,
Pyrrhias, which gives his fiery locks to fame.
The moſt atrocious of my foes was he :
Marks of his brutal violence you ſee
I bear : for as alone I chanced to ſtray
He met me in my ſolitary way,
And rudely ſeized : my ſtrength and ſpirits fly,
And, in his twelve ſtrings bound, I nerveleſs lie.”
(Plutarch *De Muſica* ; the Rev. J. H. Bromby’s tranſlation, p. 77.)

* “ I diſapprove,” ſays Ariſtotle (*Repub.* lib. viii. cap. 6), “ of all kinds of difficulties in the practice of inſtruments, and indeed in Muſic in general.   I call artificial and difficult, ſuch tricks as are practiſed at the public games, where the muſician, inſtead of recollecting what is the true object of his talent, endea- vours only to flatter the corrupt taſte of the multitude.”   The moſt important event in the early hiſtory· of Muſic was the ſeparation of muſic and poetry,

fort mufick otherwife then by unifons, octaves, and diapentes or fourths, clamming together in exact feet, I have not met with any fymptome of it before the invention and ufe of organs. And it was not poffible there could be any fuch, for the ancients did not allow thirds* and fixths to be con- cords, and without them, their fcales had no notes to found together but unifons, fourths, fifths, and eighths. And the degrees were fo defultory, that it was not poffible to bring melody and confort to joyne. They affected only the dulcer

---

which occurred in the mufical contefts added to the Pyrrhic games, at the clofe of the Criffæan war. (*Paufanias Græc.* lib. x. cap. 7.) " From this time Mufic became a diftinct art; the chorufes, which till now had governed the melody of the lyrift and tibicen, became fubordinate to both. Philofophers in vain exclaimed againft thefe innovations, which they thought would ruin the morals of the people, who, as they are never difpofed to facrifice the pleafures of the fenfes to thofe of the underftanding, heard thefe novelties with rapture, and encouraged the authors of them. This fpecies of Mufic, therefore, foon paffed from the games to the ftage, feizing there upon the principal parts of the drama, and from being the humble companion of poetry, became her fovereign." (Burney, *Hift. of Muf.* i. 426.)

* The true major third was either not difcovered or not admitted to be confonant till a very late period, Ptolemy being the earlieft extant author who fpeaks of the *minor tone* (See Burney, *Hift. of Muf.* i. 448); a fact which is fo extraordinary, and fo contrary to all that could have been anticipated, as to deftroy all confidence in any *a priori* reafoning on the fubject of counterpoint among the ancients. The pofitive evidence in its favour confifts chiefly in certain indications of two modes having been ufed at once. Thus the expreffion in Horace (*Epod.* ix. 5),

"Sonante miftum tibiis carmen lyrā
Hac Dorium, illis barbarum"

is interpreted to mean that the lyre was played in the Dorian mode, and the tibiæ in the Lydian; fo that if the *ancient* Dorian and Lydian octave were

of found as the defcriptions in authors fhew, who have ufed for a fimile, that perfons of divers tempers fhould in action agree like divers muficall notes, which founding together are pleafing to the fence. They had no imagination of counterchanging harfh & mild confonances, or four and fweet fetting one and other, &c. Nor had they any knowledge of the monarchy of a key with its full accord, nor of the leaft femple in the way of our art of compofition. It is therefore very hard to make a comparifon of fuch meer difparature as the muficall harmony of the ancient and modernes are. It may be allowed that the former might be good, but in *fue genera* not as confort, but fome what els which for want of practick examples, wee cannot judge of.

21.
Of the Theatre Mufick.

But now to come downe to the Theatres, where mufick was in its altitude. It feems the entertainment was made up of action and finging * like our operas, about which many

---

employed, the former being of the fourth fpecies, while the latter was of the fecond, and pitched two tones higher, the feries of intervals heard would confift of fourths and major thirds, or rather double tones. Again, there are paffages fuch as—

Αἰολεὺς ἔβαινε Δωρίαν κέλευθον ὑμνῶν

(quoted from Pindar by the Scholiaft on Pyth. ii. 127), which are fuppofed to indicate that poetry written in one mode and fung accordingly, was accompanied by inftruments in another. For a view of the moft that can be made of thefe arguments, fee Böckh (*De Metris Pindari*, iii. 10). Confult alfo Dr. Smith's *Dictionary of Greek and Roman Antiquities* (Article Greek Music).

    * The Greek dramas confifted of foliloquy, dialogue, and chorus; but as the chorus was never adopted in the Latin comedy, it has been imagined, that fuch *Cantica*, or foliloquies, as were full of fentiment and paffion, had a dif-

queftions may be moved. As for the action it was vifible upon the ftage, but the voices were only heard, and how could that be in an open theatre, *fub dio*, with thoufands of auditors in them? and knowing the difturbances incident to crowds, how can wee imagin the actors could make themfelves underftood? As to that I confider, firft, that they did not fpeak, as ours doe, but fung* with all the utterance of found they could make, and wee can conceive that to double the ftrength of the voice. And next, that they did no t mumble, like our comon fpeaking, but pronounced every

---

ferent, more elaborate, and refined melody and accompaniment fet to them, than the *Diverbia*, or dialogues; and that like the chorus of the Greek tragedy, they ferved as interludes or act tunes. The term *chorus* (χορος) equally means a band of fingers, and a company of dancers. Many inftances occur, however, in ancient authors, where dancing in the old drama of the Greeks, feems but another word for moving and acting gracefully; and the term *hypocritic*, which the Greeks likewife call *archefis*, and the Latins *faltatia*, though it fometimes means dancing, more frequently is ufed to exprefs gefture, or theatrical action.

* Everything was upon a large fcale in the ancient theatres. The figure, features, and voice were all gigantic. The voice was, in a particular manner, the object of an actor's care; nothing was omitted, fays Father Brumoy, that could render it more fonorous; even in the heat of action it was governed by the tones of inftruments, that regulated the intervals by which it was to move, and to exprefs the paffions. Ariftotle tells us (*Poetics*) that "Mufic formed an effential part of tragedy;" and innumerable paffages might be quoted from ancient writers, to prove that all the dramas of the Greeks and Romans were not only fung, but accompanied by mufical inftruments. The want of natural power of voice fufficient to be heard in the open air, for the ancient theatres had no cover, and by a great multitude, gave rife not only to finging upon the ftage, but, perhaps, to chanting in the church. The neceffity of augmenting the force of a performer's voice by every poffible means likewife firft fuggefted the idea of metallic mafks, which were ufed by the actors upon the principle of fpeaking trumpets, and to that of the *Echeia* or harmonic vafes.

individuall fyllable according to its quantity, fo that no confufion took place, but all the language was diftinct and clear.
And then, as Vitruvius defcribes, a circle of brafs veffels
were planted round the compafs of the theatre,* tho' I cannot
think that Pereault† hath nicked the contrivance, by fhut-
ting them up in cavaties which for the purpofe fhould ftand
open. That thefe might augment the voice is certain, but
then they muft be tuned to the quadrichord, or the general
tone in which they fung, els they would not augment at all,
nor anfwer to any fyllable that did not ftrike the true tone of
the veffels.

But as great an affiftance as all this was the chorus of

---

   * The *Echeia* or *vafes* ufed in theatres for the augmentation of found, are
defcribed by Vitruvius (book v. cap. 5). He tells us that they were placed in
cells or niches, between the rows of feats occupied by the fpectators, to which
the voice of the actor had free paffage; that they were made of brafs or earth-
enware, and proportioned in magnitude to the fize of the building; and laftly,
that in the fmall theatres, they were tuned in harmonical proportions of fourths,
fifths, and eighths, with their replicates; and in theatres of great magnitude, there
was a vafe to correfpond with every found in the difdiapafon, or great mufical
fyftem, in all the genera. The Echeia were brought firft into Italy from Corinth,
by Mummius. Vitruvius continues to thefe veffels the Greek name—*Vafa
Ærea*—*que Græcè* Echeia *vocantur*, as more expreffive of their ufe than any term
he could find in the Latin language. (See Hawkins, *Hift. of Muf.* i. 187;
Burney, *Hift. of Mufic*, i. 148.)

   † Claude Perrault, the celebrated architect and member of the Royal Academy of Sciences at Paris, was the editor of an edition of Vitruvius, publifhed
in that city in 1673. He there gives an engraving of part of an ancient theatre on
purpofe to exhibit the fituation of the harmonic vafes. Kircher has not only
defcribed, but given them imaginary forms refembling bells. (See *Mufurgia
Univerfalis*, tom. ii. p. 285.)

tibia, that founded unifon to all that was fung ;* this favoured the voices fo much that any one might performe his part with half the breath ; as every one ufed to fing in one way, with or without a full thro' bafe can tell. But I have a farther profpect of advantage, which is that the actors did not fing at all, or but as fingle perfons, and the matter of the drama was made out by chorufes of many voices, and with fo much vociferation as was eafily heard, efpecially the mufick attending. And this manner with them did not run into gabble like our fpeaking or finging together, for nothing was more facredly required then diftinction of feet and fylla- bles, in which the leaft diforder made a mutiny in the theatre. And during all this the actors might be but pantomimes, and ufed the grimace & gefture as if they fpoke, as well as acted.† If this was not fo, I defire to know to what end panto-mimikery was fo much ufed, and applauded ? To fee men act, faying nothing muft be the dulleft fight in the

---

* Athenæus has preferved a little poem by Pratinas, of the *Hyporchema* kind, where he gives vent to his indignation, on account of fome theatrical perform- ance, in which, inftead of the *tibicines* accompanying the chorus, the chorus had accompanied the tibicines : " The flute-players did not *play* to the chorus, but the chorus *fung* to the flute-players."

† The ftrange cuftom of dividing the declamation and geftures, or fpeaking and acting, between two perfons was never thought of by the Greeks. It is mentioned by Livy as an invention of Livius Andronicus an old Roman poet (B.C. 240) in order to fave himfelf the fatigue of finging in his own pieces ; to which he, like other authors of his time had been accuftomed—(*Encyclop. M. Duclos*, ART. *Declamation des Anciens*). In the younger drama, according to Lucian (*De Salutatione*) a fingle dancer or *Mime*, was able to exprefs all the in- cidents and fentiments of a whole tragedy, or epic poem, by dumb figns, but ftill to mufic, as the actors recited it.

world; complements and the like may be underſtood by drye action, but not in *eiſdem verbis*, nor anything of ſcience or reaſoning. Its true one may act and another ſpeak, and it ſhall be hard to ſay which is which; as Tully reports of Roſcius, that he was challenged to ſpeak, and Roſcius undertook to act what he ſayd, as faſt as he ſpoke it. Therefore our paltry imitators are miſtaken when they attempt to mime it upon a ſilent ſtage; but if the parts were rehearſed (near) and they acted, or (perhaps) as the ancients to a chorus, they might be accepted as the ancient mimes were.

23.
Of the Tibia
pares and
impares.

    I cannot drop this ſubject, before I have directed another bolt at the theatricall muſick of the ancients, aiming chiefly at the *Terentian* comedys which carry ſome mark of diſcovery in the ſhort inſcriptions.* It is certain they were ſung or rather toned to muſick, which were the tibia *pares* and *impares*,† as it is there expreſt; and alſo that the modes

---

   * The comedies of Terence having been accompanied by the pipe, the following notices are prefixed to explain the kind of muſic appropriate to each: *tibiis paribus*, i. e. with pipes in the ſame mode; *tib. imparibus*, pipes in different modes; *tib. duabus dextris*, two pipes of low pitch; *tib. par. dextris et ſiniſtris*, pipes in the ſame mode, and of both low and high pitch. Theſe terms have given abundance of occupation to critics and commentators, who, after all, have been unable to make anything of them.

   † After all that has been written upon the ſubject of the ancient flutes *pares* and *impares*, the moſt probable concluſion is that the terms ſignified *double* flutes *equal* and *unequal* in point of length and ſize. For in none of the repreſentations in ancient painting or ſculpture, does it appear that the tibicen, either at ſacrifices or in the theatre, plays on a *ſingle* flute, though we as often ſee double flutes of *different* lengths in his hands, as of the ſame length; and as harmony, or muſic in different parts, was not practiſed by the ancients, the flutes of equal

were made by a famed mufitian. There is nothing in the land of critifcifme more dark then the fence of thefe words, *pares* and *impares*. The tibia were pipes that founded by a reedall device like thofe affixed to bag-pipes, and foraminated for changing the tone when there was occafion. They were alfo termed *dextera* and *finiftra*,* becaufe two pipes met in an angle at the mouth, fo that to manage them, there was

length may naturally be fuppofed to imply *unifons ;* and *unequal* fuch as are *octaves* to each other. Among the Greeks and Romans it was fo ufual for a performer to play on two flutes at the fame time, that he was called *canere* or *cantare tibiis*. (*Gellius*, xv. 17 ; *Corn. Nepos*, xv. 2, § 1.) Cafpar Bartholinus, the celebrated anatomift, has written a treatife (*De Tibiis veterum et earum antiquo ufu*, Rome, 1677) in which he has brought together a great variety of intelligence refpecting the flutes of the ancients. In this work is a chapter entitled " Tibia in Ludis Spectaculis atque Comediis," where the author takes occafion to fpeak of the *tibiæ pares et impares* and alfo of the *tibiæ dextræ et finiftræ*, ufed in the reprefentation of the comedies of Terence, which he illuftrates by plates reprefenting the forms of them feverally, as alfo the manner of inflating them, taken from coins and other authentic memorials. In particular he gives an engraving from a manufcript in the Vatican library, of a fcene in an ancient comedy, in which a tibicinift is delineated ftanding on the ftage and blowing on the *tibia pares*, or two equal flutes. The *tibia pares* was ufed by the Saxons, and is depicted in an Anglo-Saxon manufcript (MS. Cott. Cleop. C. 8) in the Britifh Mufeum. It was alfo ufed in the time of Richard II. See a drawing from the *Liber Regalis*, in Strutt (*Manners and Cuftoms*, vol. ii. pl. 6). It may alfo be feen in the ancient fculptures outfide St. John's Church, Cirencefter (See Carter, *Specimens of Ancient Sculpture*, vol. ii. p. 11).

* Suppofed to have been called *dextra* and *finiftra* becaufe the former was more properly held in the right hand and the latter in the left. Herodotus (i. 17) calls them " male and female," i. e. probably bafs and treble, correfponding to the ordinary fexual difference in the human voice. The *tibia dextra* was ufed to lead or commence a piece of mufic, and the *finiftra* followed it as an accompaniment. Hence the former was called *incentiva*, the latter *fuccentiva* (Varro, *de Ruft.* i. 2.)

work for right hand and left; but that pofition making no difference the crittiques allow not the diftinction to be from thence but from the fcene; that is the right and left of the ftage; and as for the *pares* and *impares* fome will have it referre to magnitude, but there is no fymptome of inequallity of the tibia in any peice of antiquity;* others will have it to the foramina, in one odd and in the other even, by which the tones are unequall; but *pare* and *impare* belongs neither to magnitude nor founds, but to numbers onely. My thought is that after Ariftotle, and other philofofers had began to efteem harmony by numbers mathematically, then all confonances muft needs be refolved thereby, and thence all the clatter about rations, *bipartientes, fuper-bipartientes, fefquaul-teras, fefquertias,* &c. And fo according to 9th Elem. which treats of *pares* and *impares,* &c. by like analogy, fome confonances were ftyled *pares,* and others *impares.* I fhould not have ventured upon a guefs fo wide from the ordinary, if I had not found enough in Plutarch (*Eodem Interprete*) to lead

---

* Bartholinus (*De Tibiis Vet.* pl. 8) gives an inftance of an unequal double flute with plugs; one ftraight and the other curved; and tells us from Ariftotle's *Acouftics,* that loudnefs and clearnefs were acquired by the addition of the curve. In the paintings of Herculaneum, fome of the double pipes are furnifhed with pegs, fixed into the upper fide of each tube, towards the lower extremity; but it is difficult to afcertain the purpofe for which they were intended. Some have two in each; others five in the left, and feven in the right hand pipe; and others again five in the right, and none in the other, which is of much fmaller dimenfions, both in length and thicknefs. One of the laft named is depicted in Wilkinfon (*Man. and Cuft. of the Anc. Egypt.* vol. ii. p. 311). Another reprefentation of the unequal double-flute may be feen in Burney (*Hift. of Mufic,* vol. i. pl. 6.)

me into it; the words are thefe:—" *His ergo partibus atque*
" *numeris harmonia de Ariftotelis fententia componitur. Idem*
" *optiffme ex finiti et infiniti, paris et imparis atque pariter im-*
" *paris. Natura eadem conftituet ejufque partes. Tota enim*
" *par eft, cum conftet quatuor terminis partes ipfius, propor-*
" *tionibus continentur, quorum termini funt pares, impares, pa-*
" *riter impares;*" and examples follow. If I am afked if
I underftand this, I muft anfwer no, no more then the reft of
the tract. But I can tell, that the tibia *pares* and *impares*
being fo ftyled in Terence cannot be refolved according to
any of the crittiques, but muft be underftood according to
this mathematicall prefcription (fuch as it is) or not at all. If
any one would fee a collection of thefe crittifcifmes, they may
be had in Rofinus'* *Antique ;* and in the variorum Terrence,
at the beginning, there is a note of this fubject *ex profeffo.*

It is impoffible to ftate the mythologie of thefe defcriptions, without repairing to the nature of the fubject, which
onely can difcover what may or may not be intended by them.
The Theatres being open to the ftage and immenfly filled
muft require magnitude of found to make an inteligible entertainment, which was to be the comedy fung to the found
of wind mufick, called tibia, of which there were divers forts,
knowne by certain names, as *pares, impares, dextræ, finiftræ,*
and *farannæ,* mentioned in Terence, and which foever were

24. The generall difpofition of Theatre mufick.

---

* John Rofinus, an able antiquary, born in Thuringia about 1550; died
1626. His work is entitled *Antiquitatum Romanorum Corpus abfolutiffimum.*
Bas. 1585, folio. There are many editions.

ufed, muſt ſound concordant; and that could not be but as
I ſayd in uniſons, octaves, (higher or lower) fourth's or fifth's.
And this could not be otherwiſe then in counterpoint with
the voice, which was governed by the accents (*ab accinendo*),
that is recitative, with deflections as was preſcribed, and the
ever neceſſary rule cited out of Plutarch, of the ſtrickt coinci-
dence of ſound, time, and ſyllable, obſerved. And ſo the clang-
our of the muſick could not drowne the voices, but augmented
them, which was the effect of ſuch nice coincidences. And
of the pipes the uniſons and octaves to the tone of the theatre,
or the vaſæ mentioned by Vitruvius, of which the numbers
being as 2, 4, 8, 16, might make them be ſtyled *pares*, and the
fourth, as 3 to 4, or fifth, as 3 to 2, might be the *impares*; and
the dexter and ſiniſter referre to ſhapes or modes of handling
them; or, as was ſayd, to the ſides of the ſtage; and the modes
(ſaid allwaies to have bin made) might be as I gueſſed, alter-
ing the time as ſceenes changed, and ſuited the ſubject and
perſons, and perhaps ſetling the accents, or tones, of which
with other circumſtances, the nicety of thoſe times, and the
witts that courted them, from the examples of various nations
and republicks, gave occaſion for endleſs variety, and might
well render the performances no leſs admirable in their way
then the operas of our days are in our manner. And I might
ſay more worthily, and give good reaſon for it; but compari-
ſons are odious. I muſt take one thing for granted, which is
that whatever the pipes were, the ſounding part muſt be, not
like our bag-pipes without ſtop, but ſo contrived that the
tongue might comand the ſound with diſtinction of touch
preciſely like our Hautboys; els the feet and ſyllables could

not be expreft, then which in the greateft nicety of time nothing was more effentiall. But neither in the lettered or
carved defcriptions, is there any fymptome of fuch, or of any,
manner of voicing whatever.

I have fayd litle of the Diatonian tetrachord having confi-
derations concerning that which are not proper to the others ;
for in the firft place the degrees are marked out by true harmony, as nature itfelf accords it ;* and when one is fet above
another, it fullfills the feptenary, which is the treafury of
concord, and the whole becomes one fcale, of which the tones
are allyed to each other, as all are to the firft, faving that to
accomodate fome humour in finging the femitone hath bin
put firft, which in naturall order follows the two tones. It
appears that the ancienter mufitians affected this fcale, as
moft magnitick, and proper for heroicks, or the tragicall
fongs in prais of Baccus. But when the verfifying vein turned
fantafticall, and affected variety, and lyricks in comon mufick,
and comicks in the theatres, came in ufe, the other fcales fol-
lowed† and perhaps were at firft invented for fuch melodys

25.
The Diato-
nian the
ancienter
and jufter
fcale.

---

* The regular *diatonic* fcale confifted, (as we have feen,) like the modern,
of tones and femitones. The ancients attributed peculiar effects to each genus,
and fpeak of many characteriftic diftinctions of genera, which now appear to be
wholly fanciful and imaginary. Ariftides Quintilianus (edit. *Meibomius*, p. 111)
tells us that " the diatonic is manly, and auftere ;" and in another place (p. 19)
that it is the moft natural, " becaufe all who have ears, though uninftructed in
mufic, are capable of finging it."

† The *chromatic* fcale confifted of femitones and minor thirds ; and the *enharmonic* of quarter tones and major thirds ; diftinctions which feem to have
been religioufly obferved in Greece ; as the lyre was allowed but four ftrings to

as had lefs of harmony, and more of paffionate whining then
fuited with the diatonick intervalls, which difference will be
manifeft to thofe who will pleas to make a comparifon of
them.   The antiquity of the diatonian among the Greeks,
being probably the mufick of Homer, inclines me to think it
was alfo the fcale of the Hebrean, and that their polychord
inftruments were tuned accordingly, the other fcales being
the invention of the latter Greeks.

each tetrachord, and flutes were bored in a particular manner for each genus,
in which no provifion was made for producing the tones peculiar to the other
two.   Plutarch laments the difufe of the old enharmonic fcale in the following
words :—" The moft beautiful of the mufical genera, the *enharmonic*, which
on account of its grave and folemn character was formerly moft in efteem, is
now however wholly laid afide ; and there are few perfons in the prefent day,
who appear capable of difcerning the interval, which is its characteriftic.   So
obtufe are become the perceptive faculties of the generality, that the Enharmonic Diefis is affirmed to be abfolutely undiftinguifhable ; and on this affumption
it is not only denied a place in the mufical fcale, but brings on all, who favour
the ufe of it, the name of triflers.   Yet the moft formidable argument of its
opponents amounts to no more than this, that becaufe their auditory organs are
unable to difcriminate the minute divifions of the tone which the genus admits,
there is therefore no foundation for it in nature ; and it confequently ought not
to be allowed in practice.   Another argument, alfo, urged by them, is the in-
compatibility of the Diefis with fymphony ; which is not the cafe, they fay, with
the other intervals, viz. the femitone, tone, &c.   But they forget that they
ought, for the fame reafon, to difcard from practice the third, fifth, and feventh
intervals, which confift refpectively of three, five, and feven diefes.   And indeed all the uneven intervals (or thofe which contain the fmalleft diefis an uneven
number of times) ought on the fame ground to be rejected, fince none of them
can be ufed in fymphony.   It is, in fact, a neceffary refult of their doctrine,
that no divifions of the fcale are applicable to practice except thofe, in which
the intervals are expreffed by even numbers ; the intenfe diatonic, for inftance,
and the tonic chromatic." (*De Mufica*, the Rev. J. H. Bromby's tranflation,
p. 102—3.)

And that which tended moſt to revive the Diatonick muſick among the Greeks, was the increaſe of compaſs in their ſtringed inſtruments;* for ſo they roſe to a diſdiapaſon or higher, which with the proſlambomenos made a large catalogue of notes with names and ſignatures, which are ſet forth particularly in moſt authors. Theſe muſt of neceſſity lead to the knowledge and practiſe of accords, however their dutyfull ears did not allow of thirds and ſixths. And to leſſen the wonder that muſt attend ſuch miſtakes of artificiall men, I have to alledg that the numbers, the mathematick philoſofers were pleaſed to annex to thoſe accords, fell not into ſuch clever proportions, as they thought belonged to concords, and ſo the numerall elements (*annuente Pythagora*) and not the ſence of hearing muſt governe in thoſe caſes. But it is uſuall for arts to grow by degrees, and often very ſlowly, as men happen to be tenacious of old uſages. So harmony altho' it was plainely revealed by the polychord inſtruments, and probably divers of them might be uſed together in ſome ſort of conſort, yet the powers of the vocall manner was ſo great that it held muſick to the tetrachords for divers ages; and wee find in the time of Auguſtus, when Vitruvius wrote,

26.
Inſtruments
eſtabliſht
fine harmony.

---

* About the time of Sappho and Anacreon, ſeveral ſtringed inſtruments, ſuch as *magadis*, *barbiton*, and others, were uſed in Greece, and eſpecially in Leſbos. They had been introduced from Aſia Minor, and their number of ſtrings far exceeded that of the lyre, for we know that ſome had a compaſs of two octaves, and others had even twenty ſtrings, ſo that they muſt have more reſembled a modern harp than a lyre (Bode, *Geſch. der Lyriſch Dichtkunſt der Hellenen*, p. 382, &c. Compare *Quinctil.* xii. 10).

who defcribes mufick* accordingly, and is as hard to be underftood as any of the other authors of the Greek mufick. And
in that manner, that is by tetrachords, the diatonian fcale was
ufed in theatres, and ordinary finging, till the ufe of organs,
and other incidents, made a totall revolution of muficall difcipline, as I fhall fhew. But in the mean time I muft obferve, that after the grandees had a taft of inftruments in
confort, voices became more flighted, or els conformed, and
the chromes and harmonicks (for the difficulty, as authors
alledge) layd afide. Inftrumentall mufick, *poft various cafue*,
hath got ground, and downe even to our days prevails, and
voices have had much adoe to maintain their poft in muficall
entertainments.

Being come fo forward as the eftablifhment of the Roman
monarchy, there is to be obferved a vaft alteration of the
methods of knowledge in the world. The philofophy of the
Greeks, efpecially the phificall, flighted the arts mathematicall under grofs mifconftruction, and the witts refined upon
the arts of goverment and warr; but moft efpecially upon
the nicetys of oratory, and its felow poetry. Moft other
pretenfions to knowledge ceafed, and matters went foreward

---

* All that Vitruvius has written upon Mufic is contained in his work, *De
Architectura*, lib. iii. cap. 3, 4, and 5. In laying down the rules for the con-
ftruction of theatres he fpeaks of Mufic in general terms, and afterwards of the
Echeia or harmonic vafes (before mentioned) for the purpofes of reverberation.
He thence takes occafion to mention the genera of the ancients, which he illuftrates by a fcale or diagram, compofed, as he fays, by Ariftoxenus, though it does
not occur in the valuable edition of that author publifhed by Meibomius.

more majorem, onely the fluice gates of luxury were fet open, and as an ingredient in that mixture wee have reafon to fuppofe mufick to have bin entertained or rather courted. Altho' verfes were much in fafhion, and lyricks plenty, which wee may fuppofe were intended to be fung *ad lyram*, yet ordinarily, as I guefs, verfes were repeated alfo plain ; for who ever heard that among the Romans, either old Ennius, Lucilius, Horace, Sermones, Virgill, or any poems (out of theatres) were fung. And in the theatres not for the fake of the poetry, but for augmentation of voice. The witts ufed to rehears their poems in affemblys, as wee find in Pliny ; but no hint of any manner, muficall or otherwife. So that poetry and mufick, from being twinns, were fcarce fifters. There is in Quintillian* an exquifite encomium of mufick, where the originall laudable ufe, and the then moderne corruption of it, is fet forth, as being mired in the theaters, and proftituted by light weomen (*fpadicà*) with pfalters ; and in fhort, from a fober enterteinment of the wife and vertuous, was become a property of vice and intemperance. And fo wee muft conceive it proceeded, from bad to wors, till it funk in the gothick warrs, and by means of the Chriftian churches was happyly revived, or rather preferved, and thereby derived to us.†

---

* *M. Fabri Quintiliani De Inftitutione Oratoria.* There is an excellent Englifh tranflation of the *Inftitutions* by Patfall, 2 vols. 8vo. 1774.

† In Mufic as well as in other arts the genius of Greece had left little for Rome to do, but admire and imitate. The ancient Romans derived their knowledge of mufical notation, mufical inftruments, and mufical performance, both vocal and inftrumental, from the Greeks and Etrufcans. Great obfcurity,

This matter I fhall refume afterwards, but in the mean time have fome regard to the devifion of the empire. This

however, involves the ftate of Mufic among the ancient Romans. Almoft all the beft muficians at Rome feem to have been foreigners. Some writers infift that the ancient Romans had the merit of fimplifying the Greek mufical notation, by employing in its ftead the firft fifteen letters of the Roman alphabet. But this is difproved by what remains of the works of the ancient Roman writers upon Mufic. In the fourth century, the Greek mufical charaćters were in ufe, and a century later, when Boethius and Martianus Capella wrote. (See their Fragments, edited by Meibomius, *Antiquæ Muficæ Auĉtores Septem*. Elzev. 1652.) The year B.C. 365 marks an era in Roman Mufic by its adaptation to theatrical amufements. It is in this year we find mention of a *leĉtifternium*, at which aĉtors were firft brought from Etruria, who, without verfes, danced in dumb fhow to the found of the flute. Some time later, Livy (ix. 30) mentions a curious tale of the defertion of certain Roman flute-players, who were only brought back by an amufing ftratagem. We learn from Valerius Maximus (ii. 5), that the Roman flute-players were incorporated into a college, and Ovid (*Faft*. vi. 657), fpeaking of their ancient importance, fays—

     " Temporibus veterum tibicinis ufus avorum
         Magnus, et in magno femper honore fuit :
      Cantabit fanis, cantabit tibia ludis,
      Cantabit moeftis tibia funeribus."

There does not appear to be any trace of a Roman mufical fyftem entirely diftinĉt from the Greek. A paffage in Cicero would lead us to fuppofe that the laws of contraft, of light and fhade, of loud and foft, of fwelling and diminifhing, were underftood by the Romans (*De Oratore*, iii. 44), on which point there is no clear evidence to decide the queftion with reference to the Greeks. Still the Roman mufical writers, as St. Auguftin, Macrobius, Martianus Capella, Caffidorus, and Boethius, (all of whom flourifhed between the fourth and fixth centuries of the Chriftian era,) did nothing to improve the fcience of Mufic, and were little more than copyifts of their Greek predeceffors. Livy (lib. xxix. cap. 6) mentions, that after the conqueft of Antiochus, the great

fell out after Conſtantine, and it was not long before inſtead of one, there was two Rome's. The Eaſterne had a ſucceſſion of monarchs till in the year [1452] the Turks conquered Conſtantinople.* There are hiſtorians that write of this eaſterne goverment, as Mexia,† &c. who have deſcribed the portentous luxury, with the abominable wickedneſſes of thoſe courts, but no ſyllable of the muſick uſed amongſt them, either in the pallaces, or churches. Whence I may remark, that in times when men lived free and at eaſe, and which were deſervedly accounted good, muſick was a freind, and celebrated to poſterity as ſuch; but in factious, ſeditious, gluttonous and debauched times, when men did *tantum non* eat one another, muſick was made a ſlave, and tho' perpetually held in exerciſe, yet ſo ſlighted, that no remembrance of it is left to poſterity. But it is preſumed the Greek pa-

---

King of Syria, the cuſtom was firſt introduced at Rome of having *Pſaltriæ*, or female muſicians, to attend and perform at feaſts and banquets in the Aſiatic manner.

* The taking and ſacking of Conſtantinople by the Turks in the year 1452, was followed by an emigration of learning and learned men, who eſcaping from the deſtruction that threatened them, ſettled chiefly in Italy, and became the revivers of literature in the weſtern part of Europe. Theſe men, upon their removal from Conſtantinople, brought with them into Italy an immenſe treaſure of learning, conſiſting of ancient manuſcripts in all the various branches of ſcience and literature, which they diſſeminated by lectures in the public ſchools. Many of theſe manuſcripts have at different periods been printed and diſperſed, and others of them ſtill remain unpubliſhed in the public libraries and collections of Europe.

† Pedro Mexia, a Spaniſh hiſtorian of conſiderable note. His celebrated work, *Hiſtorial Imperial y Ceſarea*, was printed at Seville in 1547; at Venice in 1558; and in England in 1623.

triark and Bifhops had folemne finging in their churches, of which, together with that of the other Rome, I fhall fpeak of afterwards; but whither with or without inftruments, is no where, that I know, declared, but it's judged they ufed none. But that mufick at large receaved a great improvement in that empire I make no doubt, becaufe it is very plaine that the invention of Organs with wind (inftead of working by the force of water) was firft introduced there.*

---

* The early hiftory of the Organ is involved in much obfcurity, and has afforded ample exercife for the learning and ingenuity of mufical antiquaries. The *hydraulic* organ was acted upon by the force of water; the *pneumatic* by the application of bellows. There was no real difference in the principle, as it is only by the means of air that the pipes can produce a found. According to Athenæus (iv. 75), the firft hydraulic organ was that made by Ctefibius of Alexandria, who lived about B. C. 200. He evidently took the idea from the Syrinx or Pandean pipes, a mufical inftrument of the higheft antiquity among the Greeks. His object being to employ a row of pipes of great fize, and capable of emitting the moft powerful as well as the fofteft founds, he contrived the means of adapting keys with levers, and with perforated fliders to open and fhut the mouths of the pipes, a fupply of wind being obtained, without intermiffion, by bellows, in which the preffure of water performed the fame part which is fulfilled in the modern organ by a weight. On this account, the inftrument invented by Ctefibius was called the water organ (*Vitruv.* x. 13; Drieberg, *die pneum. Erfindungen der Griechen*, p. 53—61; Cicero *Tufc.* iii. 18). Its pipes are faid to have been of bronze and partly of reed (See Brunck *Anal.* ii. 403). It continued in ufe fo late as the ninth century of our era. Quix relates, (*Münfter-Kirche in Aachen*, p. 14,) that in the year 826, a water organ was erected by a Venetian in the Church of Aquis-granum, the modern Aix-la-Chapelle. The general form of the hydraulic organ is clearly exhibited in a poem by Publilius Optatianus defcribing the inftrument, and compofed of verfes fo conftructed, as to fhow both the lower part which contained the bellows, the wind cheft which lay upon it, and over this the row of twenty-fix pipes. Thefe are reprefented by twenty-fix lines, which increafe in

For it is reported that one of the Greek Emperors fent to his brother at Rome one of them as bigg as a chariot for a pre-

---

length each by one letter, until the laft line is twice as long as the firft. (See Wernfdorf's *Poetae Lat. Min.* v. ii. p. 394—413.)

It is generally underftood that the keys of the organ were originally fome inches wide, and played on like carillons with a blow of the fift. Be this as it may, we find that as early as the middle of the fourth century the organ was played on with the fingers—See the enigmatical Epigram attributed to the Emperor Julian (*Anthologia Græca.* Edit. Lipf. 1794, tom. iii. p. 111). The organ is faid by Platina (Lives of the Popes, p. 114 of Sir Paul Rycaud's tranflation) to have been firft employed in the public fervice of the church by Pope Vitalian, A. D. 666. Cardinal Bona (*De Divin. Pfal.* 1653) fuppofes organs to have been ufed in the church in the fourth century. Whether Vitalian was the firft to perceive the fitnefs of this divine inftrument for the fervice of the church is not quite clear, but this much is certain, that to his emiffaries Theodore and Adrian we owe its introduction into the choral fervice of the Englifh church. At the latter end of the feventh and beginning of the eighth century, the organs of the Anglo Saxons appear to have refembled even in their external decoration thofe now in ufe. The following paffage from Aldhelm (*Bibliotheca Maxima Patrum,* tom. xiii. p. 3), who died A. D. 709, will fhew that our anceftors at that time were accuftomed to gild the external pipes:

> " *Maxima millenis aujcultans organa flabris*
> *Mulceat auditum ventofis follibus ifte,*
> *Quamlibet auratis fulgefcant cætera capfis.*"

This paffage, as Mr. Sharon Turner obferves (*Anglo-Sax.* iii. 458), is alone fufficient to refute the generally received ftory of Muratori (*Art. Ital.* ii. 357), that the firft organ in Europe was that fent by the Greek Emperor Conftantine, in the year 757, as a prefent to Pepin, King of France, the father of Charlemagne. Walter Odington, a monk of Evefham, in the thirteenth century, alludes to the gift of Conftantine, in his tract " *De Speculatione Muficæ.*" He fays, that " Anno Dom. 757, venit Organum primo in Franciam miffum a potiffimo Rege Græcorum Pipino Imperatori." It alfo appears that an organ conftructed by an Arabian named Giafar, was fent to Charlemagne by the renowned " Commander of the Faithful," the caliph Haroun Alrafchid. The

sent. And the consequence of that most excellent invention
must needs be a perfection of the diatonick scale, even as wee
have it now, and that the harmony of musick must (as in time
it did) settle thereupon; but yet it seems the use of tetrachords was not quite worne out there, for I have heard some
merrily say, that the Turks in their vulgar singing, have so
much of the fourth in their emphasing as smells strong of
the tetrachord, as victors are often observed to lick up many
usages from among those they have conquered.

---

organ as it existed in the tenth century is described in some barbarous verses
written by Wulstan, a secular priest of that period, of which a portion has been
translated by Mason (*Essays on Church Music*, p. 37).ˊ Mason is however in-
correct in saying it is a " faithful description of an organ erected at Westminster."
It is the description of an organ erected by St. Elphegus, Bishop of Winchester,
in the cathedral of that city, and gives the idea of an instrument of complicated
mechanism, large dimensions, and great power. We learn that it had forty
keys, and some among them were the semitones of the chromatic scale. This
gives a compass of about three and a half octaves. It also seems probable that
the instrument was provided with a register of stops. These facts do not accord with the opinions of modern writers, i. e. that the compass of the organ
did not exceed two octaves in the twelfth century, or that half notes were invented at Venice in the same century! Prætorius tells us (*Organography*, 1615)
that the registers were not invented till towards the conclusion of the sixteenth
century. Wulstan's curious verses may be seen entire in the *Acta Sanctorum
Ordini Benedict. Sæculo*. v. p. 631-2. In the tenth century an organ was
erected with brazen pipes in the abbey church at Ramsey. The " brazen"
pipes have by modern writers been described as *brass* pipes, but we learn from
Gale (*Historia Ramenensis*, tom. iii. p. 420) that they were of copper, a metal
generally employed by our Anglo-Saxon ancestors for that purpose. According
to Mabillion and Muratori, organs became common in Italy and Germany
during the tenth century as well as in England; about which time they had
admission in the convents throughout Europe.

Now turning weſtward : as to the uſe of muſick the ſcene is little leſs deplorable. Wee allow it to have flouriſhed in the court of the latter Emperor, for in one of the auguſt hiſtorians, it is complained that the Emperor ſpent his time in his pallaces with hearing of Organs. This is the firſt notice taken of organs in hiſtory. The word *organon** is to be mett with in authors ſooner, but crittiques ſay that *organon* was a word comonly applyed to moſt muſicall inſtruments, and the *organon hydraulicon* diſtinguiſht the multifiſtular engine. And it may be depended on that this was the mother of our muſicall ſcale, and of all conſort harmony. And after the fabrick came once to be compleated, it was never in any times, good or badd, layd aſide, but numerous artiſts, that call themſelves organ builders, have ever bin, are, and probably will be imployed in the erection & voicing of them ; and all along, and yet improving, and like to be ſo to the worlds

29.
Organs
compleated.

* The term *Organum* implied the harmonical accompaniment of a chant. See the treatiſe on Muſic by the monk Hubald (written in the tenth century) preſerved in Benet College, Cambridge. John Cotton, in his valuable treatiſe, (MS. Cott. Veſpaſ. A. 2. Brit. Muſ.) after deſcribing Diaphonia as the agreement of different ſounds, ſays, " this kind of ſinging is commonly termed *Organum*, becauſe the human voice in *ſounding double* notes reſembles the effect produced by the inſtrument which is called an organ." This is a very ancient definition of the word, and puts its meaning wholly out of diſpute. Bartholomæs (*De Proprietabus Rerum*, ed. Wynkyn de Worde) ſays, " Organum is a generall name of all inſtrumentes of muſyk, and is netheleſſe ſpecyally a propyte to the inſtrument that is made of many pipes, and blowne wyth belowes. And now, holy churche uſeth only this inſtrumente of muſyk, in proſes, ſequences, and ymynes ; and forſakyth for men's uſe of mynſtralſye all other inſtruments of muſyk."

end. But as to the Greek mufick planted in the Latin empire, it is no wonder it fell, when the empire itfelf could not ftand, but was ever whelmed by deluges of barbarous nations, who became poffeffors of Italy and the neighbouring territory's and even of Rome itfelf.

30.
Poetry and
finging turn-
ed Gothick.

And in this diforder and comoniature of nations, the latine language loft its idiom, and from a vernacular fpeech became antiquarian or claffick, and the gothick dialects prevailed; and then what muft become of all the profodies and poetrys on which the mufick of former times had depended. Whenever peace returns arts will revive, as poetry, for inftance, but in a new forme, and drefs. For in Provence, as Bembo*

---

* Cardinal Bembo (*Profe, o fia della Lingua Volgare*) was of opinion that the firft rhymers and poets who wrote in a modern language were of Provence; after them the Tufcans. And both Crefcembeni (*Comment. della Volg. Poef.*) and Gravina (*Della Ragion. Poetica*) make the fame conceffion. Noftradamus, brother of the aftrologer of that name (*Les Vies des plus celèbres et Anciens Poëtes Provenfaux*, Lyons, 1575) fays that Provence was called the Mother of the Troubadours and Minftrels; and that Dante, Petrarca, Boccaccio, and other Tufcan poets enriched both their language and fancy from the productions of this country. Burney (*Hift. of Mufic*, ii. 232) fays, " During near two centuries after Guido's arrangement of the Scale and invention of the Time-table afcribed to Franco, no remnants or records of Secular Mufic can be found, except thofe of the Troubadours or Provencal poets. And though in the fimple tunes which have been preferved of thefe Bards, no time is marked and but little variety of notation appears, yet it is not difficult to difcover in them germs of the future melodies, as well as poetry of France and Italy." The time of the firft appearance of the Provencal poets has been ftated, and apparently on the authority of Crefcembeni, (*Comment. della Volg. Poef.*) to have been in the tenth century; but this is perhaps too early. The moft authentic account of them, written by Le Monge des Ifles d'Or who lived about 1248, and Henry de Saint

thinks, a new fort of verfyfying was invented, and from thence brought into Italy, and the manner, that is rimes and ftanzas, not onelly fetled there, but fpread all over Europe. This of cours introduced a new manner of finging, and that could take into no channell but that of imitating the inftrumentall mufick of thofe ages, and what that was I may reflect afterwards.

In the mean time wee muft confider what became of mufick among the Ecclefiafticks. That there was a frequent ufage of finging Pfalmes and Hymnes* from the beginning of

31.
Ecclefiafti-
call Mufick
unaltered.

Cezari, who flourifhed about 1435, two members of their own body, carries it no farther back than the twelfth century; the earlieft writer mentioned being Geoffry Rudel, Sieur de Blieux in Provence, who lived in 1161. (See a tranflation of this work, under the title of *Hiftoire des Poëtes Provencaux*, prefixed to the firft volume of *Recherches fur les Théâtres de France par M. de Beauchamps*, Paris 1735) Pafquier (*Recherches de la France*, Paris 1621, p. 600) diftinguifhes the minftrels of France from the Provencal poets by faying, that the minftrels wrote in the general language of France, as it then exifted, being a compound of the Walloon, the Latin, and Frank or German, while the Provencal poets confined themfelves to the dialect of Provence only; and fpeaking of Dante and Petrarch he remarks, that they began to write, when the Popes had eftablifhed themfelves at Avignon; before which time, Provencal poetry had been long in vogue in Provence, under the earls of Provence, and particularly under Raimond Berenger, the laft of that name. Specimens of the ancient Provencal melodies may be feen in La Borde's *Effai fur la Muf. Anc. et Mod.*; Burney's *Hift. of Muf.*; and J. S. Smith's *Mufica Antiqua*. See alfo La Borde's *Mémoires hiftoriques fur Raoul de Coucy*, 1781; Michel and Perne's *Chanfons de Chatelain de Coucy*, 1830; and the *Annuaire Hiftorique pour L'année* 1837, Paris, 1836.

* The earlieft fpecimen of a Chriftian hymn now extant is that of Clement of Alexandria, in the third book of the *Pædagogus*. On the fubject of primitive

Chriftianity, wherein confifted a great meafure of their devotion, is without all doubt; but what that manner of finging was is hard to determine, and to referre to the Jewifh pfalmody, from whence it is fuppofed to have bin derived, is *Ignotum per ignotius*. It is probable that being began by plain men, as the Apoftles were, the finging muft be as plaine, and that is a fonorous pronunciation, fyllabically, with fome turnes in the nature of accents, to which a voice, even in fpeaking, is propens. A difference might be made between the manner of finging Hymnes and Prayers, the latter with more deliberation and devotion. And fo it continued untill the eftablifhment of Chriftian churches and Bifhopricks, when great multitudes ufed to meet, and then finging was not onely for devotion, but neceffity. For without chorufes the church fervice could not be heard. And in times of calamity the Letanys were fung proceffionally about the ftreets of great citty's in divers chorufes.* Otherwife the finging in churches continued nearly in the fame manner downe to

---

Pfalmody and Hymnology, fee J. G. Baumann, *De Hymnis et Hymnopaes veteris et recentis Ecclefiæ*; J. H. Seelen, *De Poefie Chriftiana*, &c.; J. G. Walch, *De Hymnis Ecclefiæ Apoftolicæ*.

* The Litany, it is believed, was firft adopted as a proceffional fervice in the year A.D. 400. Gregory the Great, two hundred years after, in the time of a great peftilence, inftituted a fervice called the Septiformis Litania: a proceffion to different churches, compofed of feven companies of clergy, of laymen, of monks, of virgins, of married women, of widows, and of children. The proceffional performance of a part of the litany, beginning and terminating at certain fuffrages, is ftill kept up in the Roman Church, as it was in the Englifh rituals before the Reformation. See the Rev. J. Jebb *On the Choral Service of the United Church of England and Ireland*, p. 420.

about the time of Gregory, called the Great; and wee muft look abroad for the great metamorphofis of mufick that happened after the fall of the empire.

Wee muft needs imagine that after the Organ had broke the ice, and fhewed the nature and connexion of accords in mufick, that other inftruments were made to conforme in that manner, that is to a fingle fcale, without tetrachords, taking in the thirds and fixths, without which confort mufick did not fubfift. By degrees all the old inftruments conformed, or by alterations and improvement came in, and new ones invented, and brought into comon ufe. So that the harmony of inftruments fubfifted in perfection, without a dependance upon voices to recommend it. And a match was foon made between the old Harp and the Organ, which produced the Spinette kind.* For fince the Harp was to be

32.
All Inftruments conforme to the Organ.

* From all that can be gathered from ancient writers, it appears that the earlieft inftrument in which wires were acted upon by keys, was the Clavichord. It was invented by the Italians at the commencement of the fourteenth century, and was afterwards imitated by the Belgians and the Germans. It was of fquare form, and mounted with a fingle ftring only for each tone, and its mechanifm confifted of a fmall tongue of copper attached perpendicularly to the key, below the ftring upon which it was intended to act. Prætorius (*Syntagma Muficum*, p. 60) fays the clavichord was invented and difpofed after the model of the monochord. The inftrument here alluded to is fuppofed to have been one of *many* ftrings, and not the Pythagorean monochord. Julius Cæfar Scaliger (*Poëtices*, chap. 48) diftinctly traces the connection between the monochord, clavichord, harpfichord, and fpinet. The clavichord was known in England in the fifteenth century. Skelton, in his poem of *A Comely Coyftrowne* (*Pynfon* n. d.), fays of one of his characters,

" Comely he clappyth *a payre of clavycordys ;*"

touched by a plectrum, why might not the keys of an Organ be made to work the quills; and the harp itſelf gained a

---

and the writer of an old poem on muſic in the reign of Henry the Eighth has the following paſſage :—

> " Who pleythe on the harp he ſhould pley trew ;
> Who ſyngeth a ſong, let his voyce be tunable ;
> Who wreſtythe the *clavycorde*, myſtuning eſchew ;
> Who blowthe a trumpet, let his wynd be meſurabyle ;
> For inſtruments in themſelves be firm and ſtable,
> And of trowthe, would trouthe to every man's ſonge,
> Tune them then trewly, for in them is no wronge."

William Corniſh, a gentleman of Henry the Eighth's Chapel gives a ſimilar admonition in his *Treatiſe between Trouth and Informacion*, printed by Wynkin de Worde, n. d.

> " The *clavicorde* hath a tunely kynde,
> As the wyre is wreſted hye and lowe,
> So it tuenyth to the players mynde,
> For as it is wreſted ſo muſt it nedes ſhowe,
> As by this reſon ye may well know,
> Any inſtrument myſtunyd ſhall hurt a trew ſong,
> Yet blame not the *clavycorde* the wreſter doth wrong."

In the liſt of Henry the Eighth's muſical inſtruments, remaining at Weſtminſter, " in the chardge of Philipp van Wilder," immediately after the King's deceaſe (Harl. MS. 1419, f. 200) we find mention of " two payer of clavicordes." When the defects inherent in the conſtruction of the clavichord were diſcovered, a plan was deviſed of ſtriking the ſtrings with ſmall pieces of quill affixed to minute ſprings, adjuſted in the upper part of ſmall flat pieces of wood, termed *jacks*. Theſe jacks were directed perpendicularly upon the key, and when the ſpring had made its eſcape, after the ſtring had been ſtruck, the jack fell in ſuch a manner as to be able to reproduce anew the ſound at will. A ſlip of cloth applied to each ſide of the jack had the effect of a damper in ſtopping the vibration. This new invention was applied to two inſtruments, which differed only in form ; the one was the Virginal, the cheſt of which was rectan-

body of found.   But as to that and other inftruments that
found by nerves, I fhall confider afterwards.   But firft of the

---

gular, like that of fmall pianofortes; the other was the Spinet, which had the
form of a harp laid in a horizontal pofition.   The moft celebrated virginal
maker of the fixteenth century was an Englifhman, William Lewes, and among
the privy purfe expences of Henry the Eighth we find the following entry:
" Item, the vi daye paied to William Lewes for ij payer of virginalls in one
coffer with iiij ftoppes, brought to Grenewiche iii*l.*   And for ij payer of virginalls in one coffer brought to the More iii*l.*   And for a little payer of virginalls
brought to the More xx*s.*"   In MS. Harl. 1419 (before quoted), occurs this
entry : " Two faire paire of newe long virginalls made harpe fafhion, of cipres
with keis of Ivorie."   Queen Mary was celebrated for her excellent performance upon the virginals, and in a letter addreffed to her by her mother, foon
after her feparation from Henry, fhe fays, " Sometimes for your recreation ufe
your virginals and lute, if you have any ;" and by the privy purfe expences,
(publifhed by Sir Fred. Madden, 1831,) it appears that fhe was not flow in
following the Queen's advice.   Queen Elizabeth was alfo equally celebrated as
a performer, and her mufic-book is ftill preferved in the Fitzwilliam Mufeum.
A fplendid virginal, faid to have been this Queen's, is alfo in exiftence.   The
cafe is of cedar covered with crimfon Genoa velvet, upon which are three gilt
locks finely engraved; the infide of the cafe is lined with ftrong yellow tabby
filk.   The front is covered entirely with gold, having a border round the infide
two inches and a half broad.   It is five feet long, fixteen inches wide, and feven
inches deep, and is fo lightly and delicately formed, that the weight does not
exceed twenty four pounds.   There are fifty keys, thirty of ebony tipped with
gold, and the remaining twenty (i. e. the femitones) are inlaid with filver and
ivory in a moft elaborate manner.   The royal arms of Elizabeth are exquifitely
emblazoned with carmine, lake, and ultramarine, upon gold.   In an inventory
of the furniture of Kenilworth in the days of the magnificent Earl of Leicefter
(1584) we have " An inftrument of organs, regalls, and virginalls, covered with
crimfon velvet, and garnifhed with gould lace," alfo " a faire pair of *double* virginals."   And at a later period, on occafion of the " Fire Works to be prefented in Lincolnes Inn Fields on the 5th of November 1647," (a rare broad-
fide in the Britifh Mufeum) we read of virginals felf-acting, or, as the writer
expreffes it, " mufically playing of themfelves."   The virginal became fo com-

Violl kind, or Chelys as it is called, but for what reaſon I am
to ſeek.*

Nothing made ſo great a *denovement* in muſick as the invention of horſe hair, with rozin, and the gutts of animals
twiſted and dryed. I ſcarce think that the ſtrings of the old
Lyra uſed in either the Jewiſh or Greek times, which in
latine are termed nerves, were ſuch, becaus it was more or

---

mon in the ſeventeenth century, that Pepys, deſcribing the flight of the inhabitants by water at the time of the great fire, ſays, " I obſerved that hardly one
lighter or boat in three that had the goods of a houſe in, but there was a pair of
virginalls in it" (Diary, Sept. 2, 1666). This inſtrument continued in uſe until
the beginning of the eighteenth century. One of the laſt notices of it is in the
London Poſt of July 20, 1701 : " This week a moſt curious pair of virginals,
reckoned the fineſt in England, were ſhipped off for the Grand Seigneur's Sera-
glio." Galilei, in his *Dialogo della Muſica Antica e Moderna*, 1581 (p. 143), ſays,
" As the harp came from the cithara, ſo the harpſichord had its origin from the
harp ; being nothing more than a horizontal harp, as every one who examines its
figure with that idea muſt ſee." One of the earlieſt makers, if not the inventor,
of the harpſichord was Hans Rucker, of Antwerp, who flouriſhed at the end
of the ſixteenth century. He was originally a joiner, but quitting that buſineſs,
devoted himſelf entirely to the conſtruction of harpſichords, and gained a reputation which was ſurpaſſed by no other. He had two ſons, Andreas and Hans,
both equally celebrated as makers of harpſichords. The Engliſh makers of the
ſeventeenth century were Charles Haward (ſee Salmon's *Vindication of an
Eſſay*, &c. 1672, p. 68); and John Player (ſee Warren's *Tonemeter*, 1725,
p. 7).
    * The Greeks termed the ancient lyre, Chelys, from the legend that Mer-
cury formed the firſt lyre from a tortoiſe-ſhell picked up in Arcadia on a mountain called Chelydorea—See Pauſanius (*Græc.* lib. viii. *Arcad.*) Vincentio Galilei
(*Dial. della Muſica Ant. e Mod.*) has collected the various opinions of the
ſeveral Greek writers who have mentioned the invention of the chelys or
teſtudo.

lefs piacular to deal in that manner with the *entra* of dead animalls. Nor is it any where, as I know, intimated of what materiall thefe ftrings were made, but I guefs they were mettaline,* as moft fonorous, or of twifted filk; nor is there any hint when the Violl kind came firft in ufe. Had the Greeks known it, fome deity, for certain, had bin the inventor, and more worthily then Apollo of the Harp, for it draws a continuing found, exactly tuneable to all occafions & compafs, with fmall labour and no expence of breath. But as to the invention, which is fo perfectly novel as not to have bin ever heard of before Auguftulus, the laft of the Roman Emperors,† I cannot but efteem it perfectly gothick,

---

* Wire ftrings were not ufed by the Egyptians in any of their inftruments, nor, as far as we can learn from ancient authors, were they of any other quality than catgut; and the employment of this laft in the warlike bow is fuppofed to have led to its adoption in the peaceful lyre, owing to the accidental difcovery of its mufical found. There is an Egyptian lyre preferved in the Mufeum at Florence with a portion of the ftrings remaining, which are formed from the inteftines of animals. Gut ftrings are diftinctly ftated to have been ufed by Hermes or Mercury in the firft Greek lyre (Apollid. iii. 10, 2); (Diodorus, v. 75). Marpurg *Gefchichte der Mufic*, p. 17) tells us, without ftating his authority, that Linus (who according to Archbifhop Ufher flourifhed about 1280 years before Chrift) invented gut-ftrings for the ufe of the lyre, which, before his time, was only ftrung with thongs of leather, or with different threads of flax twifted together. Merfennus in his chapter *de Inftrumentis harmonicis*, prop. 11, (*Harmonie Univerfelle*, Paris, 1636,) treats largely on the ftrings of mufical inftruments, and of the fubftance of which they were formed.

† The author muft here allude to the *Chelys*, or reformed Lyre of Mercury, which according to Bianchini (*De Inftrum. Vet.* p. 28), "having the power of fhortening the ftrings by means of a neck, varied the found of the fame ftring, like feveral *magades*." Its form may be feen on an ancient vafe in the Giuftiniani collection at Rome; publifhed by Boiffard (tom. ii. p. 145) and in

and entred with thofe barbarous nations fetled in Italy, and from thence fpread into all the neighbour nations round about, and now is in poffeffion, and like to hold it, as a principall fquadron in the inftrumentall navy.

I doe fuppofe that at firft it was like its native country, rude and grofs. And that at the early importation it was of the leffer kind, which they called Viola da Bracchia, and fince the violin, and no better then as a rufhy Zampogna ufed to ftirr up the vulgar to dancing, or perhaps to folemnize their idolatrous facrifices. Thefe people made no fcruple of handling gutts and garbages, and were fo free with humane bodys as to make drinking cupps of their fculls. And when the difcovery of the vertue of the bow was made, and underftood, the *vertuofi* went to work, and modeled the ufe of it, and its fubject the viol, with great improvement, to all purpofes of mufick, and brought it to a paralell ftate with the Organ it felf. And by adapting fizes to the feverall diapafons as well above E la as the doubles below, feverall perfons take their parts, and conforts are performed with fmall trouble,

---

the laft edition of Gruter (p. 816). It was played on fometimes by the hand, and fometimes with a plectrum. See Scalig. *in Manil.* p. 384. The plectrum (a quill, or piece of ivory in imitation of one) was ufed by the ancients inftead of the bow. The oldeft traces of the viol are found in France; a fact eftablifhed by monuments of inconteftable antiquity. One of thefe is a reprefentation of an ancient French king, in the porch of the Cathedral of Notre Dame, at Paris, who holds a viol in one hand and a bow in the other. Violars, or performers on the viol, whofe bufinefs it was to accompany the Troubadours in their finging of the Provencal poetry, were common in the 12th century. See a curious figure of a Provencal Violar in Diez, *Poefie der Troubadour.*

and in all perfection. The invention needs no enconium to recomend it to posterity; for altho' it hath bin in practise many hundred years, no considerable alterations of it in forme or application have bin made which any memoriall can account for. And now no improvement is thought of or desired, but in the choice of the materiall, & curiosity of the workmanship. I shall take leave of the Violl with a remembrance onely of a merry discovery of Kircher's* in one of his windy

---

* Athanasius Kircher was born at Fulda, in Germany, in 1601, and at the age of seventeen entered the society of Jesuits. His chief work is his *Musurgia Universalis*, which is written in Latin, in ten books, occupying two volumes in folio, the first containing seven books, the second three. The subjects on which he treats are principally the following: of the propagation of sound—of the elements of practical music—of harmonics, or the ratios of sound—geometric and algebraic division of the monochord—new experiments in the construction of musical instruments—of melody, comprehending new *secrets* for producing every species of melody (!)—a parallel between ancient and modern music, pointing out the dignity of the ecclesiastical *canto fermo*, and the means of arriving at the pathetic style—of composition, or the combinations of sounds, and the application of air to poetical numbers and rhythms in all languages—musical wonders produced by hidden means, and new experiments of all kinds—and, lastly, of the various derivations of music, and the physical and artificial purposes to which it is, or may be applied. Kircher was the inventor of the Æolian harp, which he describes in his *Musurgia* (lib. ix. 352). This work, says Dr. Burney, which undoubtedly contains many curious and amusing portions, is, however, disgraced by the author's credulity and ill-founded assertions. Kircher has been truly called, " Vir immensæ quidem, sed indigestæ eruditionis" —a man of immense but undigested learning. Yet, with all its imperfections, the *Musurgia* contains much " curious and useful information for such as know how to sift truth from falsehood, and usefulness from futility ;" for a considerable portion of which, however, he was indebted to the *Harmonie Universelle* of Mersenne, which appeared in 1636; the *Musurgia* not having been published till fourteen years later.

volumes, which is a note added to the picture of a Lute and a Guittarre, that the old Hebrews ufed to found them with the fcratch of an horfetail bow !*

35.
Spinetts,
Lutes,
ftopps or
fretts, Harp
and Wind
Mufick.

As the Harpficord or Spinett kind was a compofition of the old harp and organ, fo the Lute kind is a compofition between the fpinett and the violl.   They are made of a fhape not un-like a Tortois,† which fuits with fome of the practifes (if they are not fables) of the ancients, but fo done now for con-venience of handling.   The ftopps, or fretts, of all thefe in-ftruments are a further improvement wholly unknown to the ancients, and make a diftinct inftrument with (almoft) fuffi-cient compafs, of every ftring.   But the Lute kind cannot

---

* The ancients feem to have been wholly unacquainted with one of the principal expedients for producing found from the ftrings of modern inftru-ments : this is the Bow.   It has long been a difpute among the learned whe-ther the violin, or any inftrument of that kind, as now played with a *bow*, was known to the ancients.   The little figure of Apollo, playing on a kind of violin, with fomething like a bow, in the Grand Duke's Tribuna at Florence, which Addifon and others fuppofed to be antique, has been proved to be modern by the Abbé Winckelmann and Mr. Mings.   All attempts to eftablifh the ufe of the bow among the ancients from paffages in Ariftophanes, Plutarch, and other Greek authors, have alfo proved unfuccefsful.

† It feems that in the ancient lyres the *magis*, or cavity formed towards its bafe to augment the found, was really formed of the fhell of the tortoife ; for Paufanius (*Græc.* lib. viii. Arcad.) fpeaks of a breed of tortoifes on Mount Par-thenius excellently fuited to furnifh bellies for lyres.   The belly of a Theorbo, or Arch-Lute is ufually made in the fhell-form, as if the idea of its origin had never been loft ; and the etymology of the word Guitar feems naturally de-ducible from Cithara.   The Roman C was hard like the modern K, and the Italian word *Chitarra* is manifeftly derived from *Cithara*.

ſpare the fretts as the Violl may, and in many ſhapes ſucceeds better, by plain ſtopps without them. The common Harp, by the uſe of gutt ſtrings, hath received incomparable improvement, but cannot be a conſort inſtrument becaus it cannot follow organs & violls in the frequent change of keys; and the wind muſick, which by all ſtreſs of invention hath bin brought into ordinary conſort meaſures, yet more or leſs labours under the ſame infirmity, eſpecially the cheif of them, which is the Trumpet.

Here is the furniture of the muſick ſchool, and from hence, that is from the gothick inſtitution, I fix the epoch of all our moderne harmony; all the antiq. as well vocall as inſtrumentall together with their poetry, as to theſe purpoſes, being ſunk in the pitt of Lethe. It is no wonder that the *vertuoſi* made the beſt uſe and improvement they could invent or contrive for rendring muſick compleat; and without being tyed up to the rules of proſodia and counterpoint, they ſpread their movements ſo as the parts might break one upon the other with ſufficient variety and comixtures unknowne to antiquity, and ſo farr from prejudice, that I may ſecurely add, with wonderfull and (barring ſome evil cuſtomes crept in) perfection of harmony. And all flowing as well vocall as inſtrumentall uniformely in the ſame channell without other reſtraint then the nature of things, and the comon ſence of humane kind requires. And thus thro' divers modes of operation, according to the various fancys and faſhions of different times and nations, (but all founded upon the ſame principles,) it is come downe to us, who have our turnes in de-

36.
Muſick taken a new forme.

scribing difciplinary formes as others have had : and as others before us, fo wee claim our performances to be the beft.

But now, to ftepp back a litle, wee muft confider that this revolution did not come on all at once, but gradually, and the church men were the means that brought it about; for their manner of finging the church fervices and hymnes was never according to the Greek or Latine modells, but rather after the Jewifh forme,* and they did not alter much till the

---

* In the primitive Chriftian church, the fervice confifted partly of mufic, which is fuppofed to have been chiefly that of the Greeks, with an admixture of Hebrew melody. Father Meneftrier (*Traité des Reprefentations en Mufique Anciennes et Modernes*, 1681) conjectures that the early ecclefiaftical manner of finging was like that of the ancient theatre, and Dr. Burney (*Hift. of Mufic*, vol. ii. p. 8) concurs in this opinion; but it feems much more probable that the " fongs of Zion," as performed in the Jewifh temple, and the chanting of the hymns at the Pagan altars, were chofen as vocal melodies for devotional purpofes, rather than the airs or recitatives in which the comedies of Plautus and Terence were delivered. St. Hilary, Bifhop of Poitiers, and St. Am-brofe, are faid to have been among the firft that compofed hymns to be fung in the weftern churches. Both thefe fathers flourifhed about the middle of the fourth century; but Prudentius, a Chriftian poet, cotemporary with Theodo-fius, who died in 395, was author of moft of the hymns in the Roman Bre-viary. St. Ambrofe digefted a mufical fervice for the church of Milan, which is called the Ambrofian chant, and was founded on four of the Greek modes. About the year 600, Gregory the Great enlarged and much improved the chant of the church, by the admiffion of four other modes, and gave it that form which it ftill retains in the Romifh fervice, and in which it is known by his name. Fleury (*Hift. Eccl.* tom. viii. p. 150) gives a circumftantial account of the *Scola Cantorum*, inftituted by Pope Gregory. It fubfifted three hundred years after the death of that pontiff, which happened in 604. It has been ftated that the ufage of chanting in the Englifh churches was introduced by Of-mund, Bifhop of Sarum, 1090 ; but we learn from Bede, that Benedict, Abbot

time of St. Ambrofe, who introduced the Antiphons. In thofe days Chriftians were fo numerous, and their epifcopall churches fo great and fplendid, that the prelates exalted the vocall fervices as much as they could ; and indeed it was but neceffary, for reafons touched elfwhere. It appears in Kircher and others, that there was no fteddy fcale of muficall notes till the time of Pope Gregory, who contrived the order of them by a feptenary of letters,* and Guido added the vocall fyllables, and the notation by lines, which was clumfily ex-preft before.† This was fufficient for the ufe of plain-fong

---

of Weremouth, brought Abbot John, the arch-chanter, from Rome to this country, about A. D. 678, at which period Archbifhop Theodoric, a Greek by birth, made a vifitation of the whole ifland, and caufed inftruction to be given in the art "*fonos cantandi in ecclefia*," until then known only in Kent. Bede ftates even that at an earlier period in the fame century Paulinus left at York James the Deacon, who was "*cantandi in ecclefiâ peritiffmus*," and who "*magifter ecclefiaftice cantionis juxta morem Romanorum, feu Cantuariorum multis cœpit ex-iftere*," Bede, lib. ii. 40. (See alfo lib. iv. 3, and v. 20, and the Appendix, edit. by Smith, p. 719.) The moft important treatifes on the fubject of Church Mufic are thofe of St. Nicetus in the fixth century, and Aurelian in the ninth, fubfequent to the great change introduced by St. Gregory.

* Gregory improved the notation of mufic by fubftituting the Roman letters A, B, C, D, E, F, G, and a, b, c, d, e, f, g, and aa, bb, cc, dd, ee, ff, gg, for the complicated Greek notation then in ufe. The capitals expreffed the feven founds of the loweft octave ufed for voices, and the fmaller letters the feven founds of the octave next above, while the double letters expreffed the feven founds of the next higher octave. The characters known by the appellation of *Gregorian notes* are not fuppofed to have been invented by Pope Gregory, nor were they in ufe till many ages after his time ; but fince their invention, having been appropriated chiefly to the purpofe of writing ecclefiaftical chants in the antiphonary of that pontiff, they obtained his name.

† The invention of *folmifation* is attributed to Guido, a Benedictine monk of Arezzo, in Tufcany, about the year 1022, and, although the fyftem is not

in the churches, and gave latitude enough to vary the modulations for the more fplendor of their mufick. But yet all was plain-fong, that is counterpoint unifonall, and without inequality of time, founding all fyllables of a length according to the notes. And this I take to have bin the ftate of church mufick for many years after organs and various inftruments, according to a more florid manner of compofition, by concords interwoven, called defcant, were in ufe abroad. And the churchmen having the fkill of mufick primarily amongft them, were cheifly concerned in thofe improvements, and affociated with the laity in carrying them on, by teaching, and performing with them, and probably in time learn-

wholly developed in any of his works, the teftimony of writers, very near the period in which he lived, almoft renders his claim indifputable. For an analyfis of Guido's various works, fee Dr. Burney (*Hift. of Muf.* vol. ii. p. 70, *et feq.*) and Sir John Hawkins (*Hift. of Muf.* vol. i. p. 422, *et feq.*). The invention of the *lines* and *fpaces* is certainly long anterior to the time of Guido. The learned Gerbert (*De Notis Muficis Medii Ævi Græcis et Latinis*, &c. vol. ii. p. 61) quotes a curious paffage from a chronicle of the monaftery of Corbie, in Picardy, where the writer, fpeaking of the year 986, fays, " Sub iis temporibus incœptus eft novus modus canendi in monafterio noftro, per flexuras et notas, per regulas et fpacia diftinctas, meliufculum dinumerando, quam antea agebatur : nam nullæ regulæ extabant in libris antiphonariorum et graduum ecclefiæ noftræ." This is the earlieft notice of *lines* and *fpaces* yet difcovered. The progrefs of mufical notation from the time of Pope Gregory may be traced in a few words. Gregory's method was the very fimple one of writing the words and then placing above each fyllable the letter indicating the note to which it was to be fung. Several clumfy expedients were then adopted, of writing the words on parallel lines, placing each word on a higher or lower line according to the comparative height of the found. The rudiments of the prefent fyftem are to be obferved in the method adopted about the ninth or tenth century, of drawing feven parallel lines, and expreffing the notes by *points* placed on thefe lines. At laft, the

ing from them, who might become more florid and ayery then themfelves. Thefe exercifes, which at firft were cheifly of voices, at length took in the organ and other inftruments, but (very improperly) confined their fkill to the Guidonian fcale, and made the church plain-fong the ordinary fubject. No wonder therefore that organs and other inftruments, with the defcant manner at laft entered the churches.

Nothing fhewed the influence of the ecclefiafticks over the fpirits of the laity in thofe times more then the impofition of the church plain-fong in almoft all their figurante muficke; from whence it was at firft derived, and continued downe

38.
Of Defcanting and In Nomines.

lines were reduced to four, and points placed not only on the lines, but in the fpaces between them. In more modern times it was found more convenient to ufe five lines in place of four. In Gerbert's work, *Du Cantu et Mufica Sacra*, may be found many curious fpecimens of the notations belonging to different centuries. *Id.* p. 57, curious uncial characters, and various notes and lines, to be found in many of the church-fervice books of the eighth, ninth, and tenth centuries. Plate iv. mufical characters of the tenth century, horizontally placed, ftrongly refembling thofe afterwards introduced into modern notation. Page 61, two fingular diagrams of old notation, as given by Kircher: the one, of *Greek* notation, from a manufcript of the library of the monaftery of the Holy Saviour, at Meffina, in Sicily, which manufcript, from the date (A. D. 950), would go much further back than Guido's time. In this diagram, the mufical notes are expreffed upon eight lines by means of eight letters at the beginning, and by round black dots upon the lines. The other diagram given by Kircher is from fome very ancient antiphonaries (ftill exifting) of the monaftery of Vallambrofa, in which there are points or dots upon two lines only. Further information, and examples, may be feen in Burney (*Hift. of Muf.* vol. ii. p. 35, *et feq.*) and Hawkins (*Hift. of Muf.* vol. i. p. 461, 2). See alfo a curious notice of the ancient fyftems of notation in the *Inftructions du Comité Hiftorique. Collection de documents inedits*, 1839.

beyond the Reformation, and fo near to our times, which muft be afcribed to cuftome rather then any authority. But it is fure enough that the early difcipline of mufick in England was with help of the gamut to fing plain-fong at fight, and moreover to defcant,* or fing a confort part at fight, alfo with fuch breakings, bindings, & cadences, as were harmonious and according to art; and this not of one part onely, but the art was fo farr advanced that divers would defcant upon plaine-fong extempore together, as Mr. Morley fhews;† and this exercife was performed not onely by voices and extempore, but whole conforts for inftruments of four, five, and fix parts, were folemnly compofed, and with wonderfull art and invention, whilft one of the parts (comonly in the midle)

---

* The term Defcant, in its original fenfe, fignified an extemporaneous fong, which was no fooner uttered than loft; but it was afterwards applied to the art of compofing in feveral parts. In Skelton's poem, *The Bouge of Court*, Riot is characterized as a rude, diforderly fellow, and one that could " defcant" upon any occafion—" Counter he could *O Lux* upon a potte"—that is, he could make extempory divifions upon the ancient hymn, " O Lux beata trinitas," even in his cups. Tigrini, in his *Compendio della Mufica*, Venice, 1588, fpeaks of extempory defcant upon a plain-fong as being ftill practifed in the churches of Italy. At p. 113 of the fame work, he gives inftruction in this fpecies of mufical *divination*. The moft ancient treatifes on defcant extant are thofe of Lyonel Power and Chilfton (MS. Lanfdowne, 763).

† The fecond part of Thomas Morley's *Introduction to Practical Mufick*, 1597, is entirely devoted to the fubject of defcant; and in enumerating the various compofers who have excelled in writing a number of parts upon a plain-fong, he fays, " M. George Waterhoufe furpaffed all who ever laboured in that kind of ftudy." In the Public Library, Cambridge, (Dd. iv.—60) are preferved " Mr. Waterhoufe's fongs of two parts in one upon the plain-fong of Miferere 1163 ways, in fcore."

bore onely the plain-fong thro' out. And I guefs that in fome time litle of other confort mufick was coveted or in ufe. But that which was ftyled *In nomine** was yet more remarkable, for it was onely defcanting upon the eight notes with which the fyllables (*In nomine domine*) agreed. And of this kind I have feen whole volumes,† of many parts, with the feverall authors names infcribed. And if the ftudy, contrivance, and inge-nuity of thefe compofitions, to fill the harmony, carry on fuges, and interfpers difcords, may pafs in the account of

---

* Before the introduction of the *Fantafy* in parts, the moft popular inftru-mental compofition in England was the *In Nomine*, fo called from its being founded upon an ancient ecclefiaftical chant, confifting of feven notes anfwering to the fyllables *In Nomine Domini*. The air of this chant was always preferved in one of the parts (generally the tenor), and was performed in long drawn-out notes, whilft the other inftruments executed, at the fame time, paffages in rapid divifion. Dr. Burney derives the chant from that part of the mafs beginning " Benedictus qui venit in nomine Domini ;" Sir John Hawkins, from the nine-teenth Pfalm in the Vulgate, " Lætabimur in falutari tuo : et in nomine Dei noftri magnificabimur." (See more in the Editor's Introduction to Gibbon's *Fantafies of three Parts*, publifhed by the Mufical Antiquarian Society.)

† One of thefe volumes, formerly in the poffeffion of the North and L'Ef-trange families, is now in the Editor's library. It confifts of " In Nomines and other Solfainge Songes of 5, 6, 7, and 8 partes, for Voyces or Inftru-mentes," by Robert Johnfon, Tye, Shepherd, Mundy, Phillips, Malery, Stro-gers, Tallis, Byrd, Taverner, Clement Woodcock, &c. Butler, in his *Prin-ciples of Mufic*, 1636, p. 91, fpeaks in terms of high commendation of the *In Nomines* of Parfons, and alfo of thofe of Tye and Taverner. In the Life of Milton, by his nephew Phillips, prefixed to the Englifh tranflation of his State Letters, it is faid, that John Milton the father, who was fo eminently fkilled in mufic as to be ranked among the mafters of the fcience in his time, compofed an *In Nomine*, for which he received from a Polifh prince a prefent of a gold chain and medal.

ſkill, no other ſort whatſoever may pretend ſo more. And it is ſome conformation that in two or three ages laſt bygone the beſt private muſick, as was eſteemed, conſiſted of theſe.

I would not have it thought that, by what is here obſerved, I am recomending this kind of muſick; for in one principall article, nothing can be more defective, and that is variety or what is called air. I might mention other imperfections, but that is enough. It is a ſort of harmonius murmer, rather then muſick; and in a time, when people lived in tranquillity and at eaſe the entertainment of it was aggreable, not unlike a confuſed ſinging of birds in a grove. It was adapted to the uſe of private familys, and ſocietys; and for that purpoſe cheſts of violls,* conſiſting of two trebles, two means,

---

* A cheſt of viols generally conſiſted of ſix in number, and were uſed for playing *Fantaſies* in ſix parts. A particular deſcription of their tuning may be ſeen in John Playford's *Introduction to the ſkill of Muſick*, 1655. Old Thomas Mace, in his humorous and inſtructive work, *Muſick's Monument*, 1676, p. 245, ſays, "Your beſt proviſion (and moſt compleat) will be a good cheſt of viols, ſix in number (viz.), 2 baſſes, 2 tenors, and 2 trebles, all truly and proportionably ſuited. Of ſuch there are no better in the world than thoſe of Aldred, Jay, Smith, yet the higheſt in eſteem are Bolles and Roſs (one baſs of Bolles' I have known valued at 100*l.*), theſe were old, but we have now very excellent workmen, who (no doubt) can work as well." In a collection of airs entitled *Tripla Concordia*, publiſhed in 1667, by John Carr, is the following advertiſement, "There is two Cheſts of Violls to be ſold, one made by Mr. John Roſs, who formerly lived in Bridewell, containing 2 trebles, 3 tenors, and one baſſe: The cheſt was made in the year 1598. The other being made by Mr. Henry Smith, who formerly lived over againſt Hatton houſe, in Holbourn, containing 2 trebles, 2 tenors, 2 baſſes: The cheſt was made in the year 1633. Both cheſts are very curious work." At the beginning of

and two bafes were contrived to fulfill the parts, and no thro'-
bafe* (as it is called) was then thought off—That was re-

---

the laft century, " chefts of viols" were fo completely out of fafhion that Dr.
Tudway, in a letter to his fon (Harl. MS.), thus defcribes them. " A cheft
of viols was a large hutch, with feveral apartments and partitions in it; each
partition is lined with green bays, to keep the inftruments from being in-
jured by the weather; every inftrument was fized in bignefs according to the
part played upon it; the leaft fize played the treble part, the tenor and all other
parts were played by a larger fized viol; the bafe by the largeft fize. They
had fix ftrings each, and the necks of their inftruments were fretted. Note: I
believe the treble-viol was not higher than G or A in alt, which is nothing
now."
    * The term Baffo Continuo, General Bafs, or Thorough Bafs, though now
generally confounded with Figured Bafs, and underftood to be the fame thing,
was at firft diftinct. Ludovico Viadani, of Milan, was the firft in Italy who
made ufe of the *continued* or thorough bafs. In the preface to his *Centi Con-
certi Ecclefiaftica*, Venetia, 1603, he informs us that he invented thefe pieces in
1597, at Rome, and that his chief reafon for compofing them, was that " there
were no pieces of the kind conftructed for one, two, and three voices, with an
organ bafs." In thefe concertos the organ bafs runs throughout each piece
without the flighteft paufe; it was therefore properly termed a *continued* or
thorough bafs; but it has no figures. Although it is faid that the art of figured
bafs took its rife in Italy, yet we have evidence of its practice in the Netherlands
before the beginning of the feventeenth century. Richard Deering, our own
countryman, publifhed at Antwerp, in 1597, *Sacræ Cantiones quinque vocum cum
baffo continuo ad Organum*, wherein the figure 6 is ufed wherever that chord
occurs. From this it is evident that the practice of ufing figures to a *continued
bafs* crept in imperceptibly. Ludovico Viadani was the author of a work, entitled, *Opera omnia Sacrarum Concertuum cum baffo continuo et generali, organo
applicato, novaque inventione pro omni genere et forte cantorum et organiftarum ac-
commodata. Adjuncta infuper in baffo generali hujus novæ inventionis inftruc-
tione et fuccincta explicatione Latine, Italice et Germanice.* This work is ftated
to contain *rules* for the performance of a *thorough bafs*, but the Editor has not
been able to confult a copy. It was firft printed at Venice and Franckfort in
1609; fubfequent editions appeared in 1613 and 1620. Galeazzo Sabbatini, in

ferved to other kinds of mufick I fhall mention. But this began before organs came into churches, and while the pure plain-fong prevailed in them. And then the moft celebrated forms came into fecular ufe, and fo continued in credit, in England at leaft, downe fo low as the reigne of K. Charles I. which I can judge by fome plain-fong conforts I have feen of fo late compofure. But in our days, nothing can be more monftrous and infupportable then fuch a confort would be, fo mighty is the power of cuftome and fafhion in mufick. Nor doe I pretend that the whole muficall imployment was reftrained to thefe formes, for at the fame time even from the firft launching of defcant, pieces of mufic were compofed in

---

his *Regola facile e breve per fugnare fopra il Baffo continuo nell' Organo, Monocordo, o altro fimile ftrumento*, Venetia, 1628, is ftated, to claim the *invention* of figured baffes; a miftake which has arifen from the heading of the firft chapter, " *Intention* of the author" having been read " *Invention* of the author." The practice of figuring baffes became common about the year 1623, as appears from feveral works in the Editor's collection, particularly *Madrigali Concertati a due, tre, e quattro voci, per cantar, e fonar nel clavecembalo, chitarone, ò altro fimile inftrumento, Di Zelippo Bonnaffino Meffinefe.* In Meffina Appreffo Pietro Brea MDCXXIII.; in which the bafs part is figured throughout. The harmonical combinations are, befides the common chords without figures, the chords of the 6th, the 5-6, the 6-5, and the fufpenfions of the 4-3 and 7-6. The accidental fharp third is indicated as at prefent with the fharp over the bafs note, without a figure. The earlieft work printed in England with a figured bafs is Martin Pierfon's *Motteéts or Grave Chamber Mufique*, W. Stanfby, 1630. The firft mufician who drew up rules in this country for the performance of figured baffes was William Penny, who in 1670 publifhed his *Art of Compofition, or Directions to play a Thorow Bafs*—See Clavel's *Catalogue of Books printed in England* for that year, and H. Playford's *General Catalogue of Mufick-books* (Harl. MS. 5936, No. 443). Matthew Locke's *Melothefia or certain General Rules for playing on a continued Bafs*, 1673, has hitherto been confidered the earlieft book of the kind.

different ftyles, and for various purpofes, as for merriment, and dancing, &c.,* which need not much to be inquired after. But thus farr is materiall, the earlyer conforts were compofed for 3, 4, & more parts, for fongs in Itallian or Latine out of the Pfalmes, of which I have feen divers, and moftly in print, with the names of the *patroni* infcribed.† And in England when compofers were fcarce, thefe fongs were copyed off, without the words, and for variety ufed as inftrumentall conforts, with the firft words of the fong for a title. And of this printed mufick, vocally performed, many will fhine againft the beft moderne compofitions, and I fuppofe inftrumentally would not loofe much of their excellence. And as alterations with endeavour to advance are continually profered, fo the Itallian mafters, who alwais did, or ought to

---

* " Of Vocal Mufick made for the folace and civil delight of man, there are many different kinds; as namely, Madrigals, in which fuges and all other flowers of figurate Mufick are moft frequent. Of thefe you may fee many fets of 3, 4, 5, and 6 parts, publifhed both by Englifh and Italian authors. Next, the Dramatick, or Recitative Mufick; which (as yet) is fomething a ftranger to us here in England. Then Canzonets, Vilanella's, Airs of all forts; or what elfe Poetry hath contrived to be fet and fung in Mufick," &c.—Chrif topher Simpfon's *Compendium of Practical Mufick*, 1667, p. 139. It is fomewhat fingular that the Hon. Roger North, in the courfe of thefe " Memoires," does not once allude to that delightful ftyle of compofition, the Madrigal. Its reign indeed was but brief, extending only (according to the dates of the printed copies) from 1588 to 1632; but ftill we can fcarcely conceive it poffible that its ufe was entirely laid afide in our author's *younger* days. Such however muft have been the cafe, or it certainly would have received fome notice from one fo diligent in mufical enquiries. See Oliphant's *Mufa Madrigalefca* and the Editor's *Bibliotheca Madrigaliana* for full information upon this fubject.

† The writer here alludes to the dedications which appear to nearly all the original copies of the motetts and madrigals of the 16th and 17th centuries.

lead the van in mufick, printed peices they called Fantazias,* wherein was air & variety enough; and afterwards thefe were imitated by the Englifh, who working more elaborately, improved upon their patterne, which gave occafion to an obfervation, that in vocall, the Itallians, and in the inftrumentall mufick, the Englifh excelled.†

40.
About Henry 8. Mufick began to flourifh.

For want of regifters or memorialls of times, wee can fcarce affert any thing cronically of mufick, which is wholly deftitute of thofe advantages, which few other arts want. But if one may guefs, Church mufick was at its perfection in the reigne of Henry viii.‡ He was a lover, and they fay

* See the Editor's Introduction to Orlando Gibbons' *Fantazias*, printed for the Mufical Antiquarian Society.

† Chriftopher Simpfon (*Compendium of Practical Mufick*, 1667, p. 145) fays, "You need not feek outlandifh Authors, efpecially for Inftrumental Mufick; no Nation (in my opinion) being equal to the Englifh in that way; as well for their excellent, as their various and numerous Conforts, of 3, 4, 5 and 6 Parts." Matthew Locke, in the curious preface to his *Little Confort of three Parts*, 1656, has the following paffage: "And for thofe Mountebanks of wit, who think it neceffary to difparage all they meet with of their own country-men's, becaufe there have been and are fome excellent things done by ftrangers, I fhall make bold to tell them (and I hope my known experience in this fcience will inforce them to confefs me a competent Judge) that I never yet faw any Forain Inftrumental Compofition (a few French Corants excepted) worthy an Englifh man's tranfcribing."

‡ The hiftory of the Englifh fchool of Church Mufic has never received proper attention. The accounts given by Burney and Hawkins are meagre and unfatisfactory, and all that has been written fince has only tended to involve the fubject in greater confufion. The difficulty of accefs to ancient documents, and the deftruction of the *original* part-books of our cathedrals, have confpired to render the fubject one of great difficulty. The Editor has now devoted many

compofed Anthems.*　In fome times royall familys were all fighters, and in others all fcollars : for as he was learned, fo

---

years to refearches connected with our ancient cathedral mufic, and the refult will foon be laid before the public in a work to be entitled *The Choral Mufic of the Reformation*.

* According to Hall (*Chron. An.* 2, *Henry VIII.*), the King exercifed himfelf daily in " fhotyng, finging, daunfyng, wraftelyng, cafting of the barre, playing at the recorders, flute, virginals, and in fettyng of fonges, makyng of ballettes, and did fet ii goodly maffes, every of them fyve partes, which were fong often-times in hys chapel, and afterwardes in diverfe other places." Hollingfhed has alfo a paffage to the fame effect (fee *Chron.* iii. 806). Lord Herbert of Cher-bury tells us (*Life of Henry VIII.*) that " his education was accurate, being def-tined to the Archbifhoprick of Canterbury, during the life of his elder brother, Prince Arthur. By thefe means, not only the more neceffary parts of learning were infufed into him, but even thofe of ornament, fo that befides being an able Latinift, Philofopher, and Divine, he was, (which one might wonder at in a King) a curious Mufician ; as two entire maffes compofed by him, and often fung in his chapel, did abundantly witnefs." Sir John Hawkins fays (*Hift. of Muf.* vol. ii. p. 533) that Henry VIII. " not only underftood mufic," but " was deeply fkilled in the art of practical compofition." In a collection of anthems, motets, and other church offices, in the hand-writing of John Baldwin, of the Chapel Royal, which collection appears to have been completed in 1591, is a compofition for three voices, fubfcribed *Rex Henricus Octavus*. The words beginning " *Quam pulchra es et quam decora*," are taken from the *Canticum Canticorum*, and are fuppofed to have been addreffed by the King to one of his favourite females, whom, in his early years, he had under his protection at Greenwich (See Puttenham's *Arte of Englifh Poefie*). The compofition is printed in Hawkins (*Hift.* ii. 534). *The Kynges Ballad*, beginning " Paffetyme with good company," is preferved (with the mufic in three parts) in the Britifh Mufeum (*Add.* MSS. 5665). The anthem, " O Lord the maker of all thing," compofed by William Mundy, is incorrectly attributed to Henry VIII. in the Tudway Collection (*Harl.* MS. 7339), and in Boyce's *Cathedral Mufic* (vol. i. p. 1). The miftake, according to Dr. Croft (Preface to *Divine Harmony*, 1712) originated with Dr. Aldrich. The words occur in Henry the Eighth's Primer, which probably led to the error. The mufic is attributed to Mundy in

he bred all his children to learning, and alſo to muſick, as ſome of the Hiſtorys ſhew. Queen Elizabeth* had a good touch on the Harpſicord, and Organ, and *ſub deo* confirmed the muſick in churches upon the Reformation,† which the

---

a MS. ſet of part-books formerly belonging to the Chapel of Edward VI. and in many part-books of the ſixteenth and ſeventeenth centuries. It is alſo printed with Mundy's name as the compoſer in John Barnard's *Firſt Booke of Selected Church Muſic*, 1641. The " ii goodly maſſes," mentioned by Hall as the compoſition of the royal tyrant, are not known at the preſent time. Muſic ſeems not to have been omitted in the education of Henry's ſucceſſors. See Cardan's character of the young Prince Edward VI. (Burnet, *Hiſt. of the Re-form.* part ii. p. 2), and the young King's own journal in the Britiſh Muſeum. Queen Mary was a proficient on the virginals and lute. She was taught by Mr. Paſton on the former, and by Philip Van Welder on the latter. (See *The Privy Purſe Expenſes of the Princeſs Mary*, edited by Sir Fred. Madden, 8vo, 1831.)

   * Elizabeth, as well as the reſt of Henry the Eighth's children, and indeed all the Princes of Europe at that time, had been taught muſic in early life. Camden (*Annales*, 1635, p. 6), in giving an account of her ſtudies, ſays, that " ſhe underſtood well the Latin, French, and Italian tongues, and was indifferently well ſeen in the Greek. Neither did ſhe neglect Muſicke, ſo far forthe as might become a Princeſſe, being able to ſing, and play on the lute prettily and ſweetly." Playford (*Introduction to Muſick*, Preface, edit. 1670), tells us that " Queen Elizabeth was not only a lover of this divine ſcience (Muſic), but a good proficient therein ; and I have been informed (ſays he) by an ancient muſician, and her ſervant, that ſhe did often recreate herſelf on an excellent inſtrument called the *poliphant*, not much unlike a lute, but ſtrung with wire." There is reaſon to conclude that ſhe continued to amuſe herſelf with muſic many years after ſhe aſcended the throne. See Sir James Melvil's account of her performance on the virginals (*Memoirs*, 2nd edit. Edinb. 1735). There is a curious account of Queen Elizabeth's ſkill on the virginals, in Vandernoodt's *Theatre, wherein he repreſented as wel the miſeries and calamities that follow the voluptuous worldlings, as alſo the great joyes and pleaſures which the faithful do enjoy.* Lond. 1569.

   † In 1559, Queen Elizabeth publiſhed injunctions for the clergy in the 49th,

brutallity of the Puritans would have throwne out, as the more brutall rebbells, in Charles the firſt's time actually did. But now taking a ſtand (Reg. Hen. 8.), and looking backwards for ſome time, & then forewards downe to Reg. Jac. 1, there will be ſmall ſhow of ſkill in muſick in England except what belonged to the Cathedrall Churches, and Monaſterys (when ſuch were), and for that reaſon the conſortiers wherever they went (from Minſters, as the word was), were called Minſtrels,* and then the whole faculty of muſick the

of which there is one for choral muſic. See Sparrow's *Collect. of Articles, Injunctions, and Canons,* 1684, and Heylin, p. 289.

* The word *Minſtrel* does not appear to have been in uſe here before the Norman Conqueſt; but it had long before that time been adopted in France. *Mineſtrel,* ſo early as the eighth century, was a title given to the *Maeſtro di Capella* of King Pepin, the father of Charlemagne; and afterwards to the Coryphæs, or leader of any band of muſicians. (Vide Burney, *Hiſt. of Muſic,* ii. 268.) This term *Meneſtrel, Meneſtrier,* was thus expreſſed in Latin, *Miniſtellus, Miniſtrellus, Miniſtrallus, Meneſterellus,* &c. (Vide *Gloſſ.* Du Cange and Supplem.) Minſtrels ſometimes aſſiſted at divine ſervice, as appears from a record of the 9th of Edw. IV. (See Rymer's *Fœdera,* xi. 642.) By part of this record it is recited to be their duty " to pray (*exorare,* which it is preſumed they did by aſſiſting in the chant, and muſical accompaniments, &c.), in the King's chapel, and particularly for the departed ſouls of the King and Queen when they ſhall die, &c." The minſtrels derived their knowledge from the ſchools belonging to the monaſteries. They learnt ſomething of the theoretical principles of Muſic, the practical part of ſinging, and the elements of grammar; including alſo perhaps, as much knowledge of poetry as was ſufficient for the compoſition of a ſong or ballad. Perſons already acquainted with the principles of Muſic, could find little difficulty in acquiring ſufficient ſkill to play on the viol, or ſome ſuch inſtrument, a ſimple melody; and the whole of this together formed a ſufficient body of theoretical ſcience and practical ſkill, to enable them to compoſe and play a variety of ſimple tunes. Like the eccleſiaſtics, theſe men muſt have been diſguſted with the monotony of church muſic; and

minftrelfie. And the word is (nearly) fo interpreted by Howell in his Etymologys, and by Minfheu in his Spanifh Dictionary. And as for corporation and mercenary mufick, it was cheifly flabile, and the profeffors, from going about the ftreets in a morning, to wake folks, were, and are yet, called Waits,* quafi Wakes. And that kind of mufick did not ill fuit the minftrells, becaus wind mufick was frequently ufed in churches inftead of voices, or elfe to enforce the chorus.† But in the reigne of King Jac. I., and the paridi-

---

that difpofition to hilarity and merriment which they appear to have poffeffed, would naturally lead them to the compofition of gay and lively melodies ; a method known to thofe fkilled in church mufic, by the name of Defcant. Extending their fkill ftill further, they at length formed melodies of more originality, and became in time the fole authors of the mufic, as well as of the words, of the compofitions which they fung and played. For full information concerning the ancient minftrels, fee Percy's *Reliques of Ancient Englifh Poetry;* Ritfon's *Ancient Songs and Ballads;* J. S. Hawkins' Preface to Smith's *Mufica Antiqua;* Botfield's *Manners and Houfehold Expences of England,* &c.

     * Butler (*Principles of Mufic,* p. 93), fays, " Wayghtes or Waits are Hautbois." It is remarkable of this noun that it has no fingular number ; for we never fay a Wait, or the Wait, but the Waits. In the *Etymologicum* of Junius the word is ufed to fignify the players on thefe inftruments, and is thus explained : " Waits, liricines, tibicines, citharædi, f. à verb to wait, quia, fc. magiftratus and alios in pompis inftar ftipatorum, fequantur, vel à G. guet, vigilia, guetter, quia noctu exubia agunt quæ eandem agnofcunt originem ac noftrum watch, vigiliæ. Skin." In the account of the *Privy Purfe Expences of Henry VIII.* (publifhed by Sir Harris Nicolas in 1827) are two curious entries of payments to the " wayts of Caunterbury." This is perhaps the earlieft inftance known of the ufe of the word, in the fenfe of nocturnal muficians, as Archdeacon Nares does not cite any older authority than Beaumont and Fletcher. They appear to have played to the King whilft at Canterbury, on his route to Dover, on the 9th of October, and on his return the 18th of November, 1532.

     † In the ftatutes of Canterbury Cathedral, provifion is made for players on

ficall part of the reign of King Cha. I., many muſick maſters roſe up and flouriſhed.

Their works lay moſt in compoſitions for violls; but at that time the Lute was a monopoliſt of the ayery kind, and the maſters, gentlemen and ladyes, for the moſt part uſed it. And the leſſons for that inſtrument were uſually broke into ſtrainſs, two to a leſſon, were it ayre, courant, &c.* but for pavins,† or more ſerious leſſons, three. And then the muſick

41.
The Lute enlivened Muſick which improved to Reg. Car. II.

Sackbuts and Cornets, which on high feſtivals might probably be joined to, or uſed in aid of the organ. Roger North in his *Life of the Lord Keeper* (p. 279), ſpeaking of the Cathedrals of York and Durham, ſays, "In theſe Churches wind muſic was uſed in the choir; which I apprehend might be introduced at firſt for want of voices if not of organs; but as I hear, they are now difuſed. To ſay the truth nothing comes ſo near, or rather imitates ſo much, an excellent voice, as a cornet-pipe; but the labour of the lips is too great, and it is ſeldom well founded." Matthew Lock (*Preſent Practice of Muſick Vindicated*, 1673, p. 19), ſays, "For above a year after the opening of His Majeſty's Chappel, the orderers of the Muſick there were neceſſitated to ſupply the ſuperior parts of their muſick with cornets and men's feigned voices, there being not one lad for all that time capable of ſinging his part readily."

* The moſt celebrated inſtruction book for the Lute was that publiſhed by Adrian Le Roy at Paris, about the year 1570. It was tranſlated into Engliſh, and printed by Jhon Kingſton, in 1574. A ſimilar work, by an Engliſh muſician, John Alford, appeared as early as the year 1568. Specimens of the various kinds of Lute leſſons may be ſeen in theſe works, and in *A New Booke of Tabliture for the Lute*, W. Barley, 1596; and Thomas Robinſon's *Schoole of Muſicke*, T. Eſte, 1603.

† "A *Pavan*," ſays Chriſtopher Simpſon (*Compendium of Practial Muſick*, 1667, p. 143), "be it of 2, 3, 4, 5, or 6 parts, doth commonly conſiſt of three ſtrains; each ſtrain to be play'd twice over." The name is probably derived from the city of Padua, where the tune is ſaid to have been invented.

masters fell to imitation of these, for after the Fancys, in which they had some ayre, they added a suit of lessons called Ayres, Galliards,* or other conceipts. The violin was scarce knowne† tho' now the principall verb, and if it was any where seen, it was in the hands of a country croudero, who for the portability served himself of it. And in this state, when the troubles came foreward, and the whole Society of the masters in London were turned adrift, some went into the

* " Next in course after a *Pavan* (says Simpson) follows a Galliard, consisting sometimes of two and sometimes of three strains." It was so called from the country, Gallia, whence it came.

† The Violin was in use among the common people of England at a very early period. Representations of Saxon and Norman violins occur in Strutt's *Manners and Customs.* Upon the grand door of Barfreston Church in Kent, which is of Norman architecture (probably of the eleventh century), there is the figure of a man playing upon the violin; and in the sculptures outside St. John's Church at Cirencester, is depicted a minstrel playing upon a violin with three strings. (See Carter, *Ancient Specimens,* &c. vol. ii. p. 11.) A curious representation of an Anglo-saxon concert may be seen in the British Museum. (MS. *Cott.* Tib. c. 6.) One musician has a harp of eleven strings, which he holds with his left hand, while he plays with his right; another is playing on a violin of four strings with a bow: another blows a short trumpet supported in the middle by a pole, while the fourth is in the act of sounding a curved horn. The only representation of a Norman concert is that sculptured on a double capital in the Chapter house of St. Georges de Bocherville. (See Dawson Turner, *Tour in Normandy,* vol. ii. p. 13.) Much valuable information, upon the subject of the ancient violin has been collected together by M. L'Eveque de la Ravilliere (*Poesies du Roi de Navarre,* tom. i.). See also Millin, *Antiquites Nationales,* tom. iv; the *Neu Rheinishe Mercur* for 1819, p. 19; and a valuable Essay on the History of the Violin by G. C. Anders, printed in the " Cecilia," for 1832. The latter essay is illustrated with thirteen figures of violins of the 16th century, taken from the *Musica Instrumentalis,* published by Martin Agricola in 1542.

armyes, others difperfed in the countrys and made mufick for the confolation of the cavalier gentlemen. And that gave occafion to divers familyes to entertein the fkill and practife of mufick, and to encourage the mafters to the great increas of compofition. And this good humour lafted fome time after the happy Reftauration, and then decayed, which with the reafons may be difcourft of afterwards.

In the reigne of King James the firft mufick had the greateft encouragement, for the mafques at Court,* which were a fort of Balles, or Operas, found imployment for very many of them, and in the Theaters at Court they were adorned with liverys, that is divers coloured filk mantles and fcarfs with rich capps, and the mafter in the fhape of an Appollo,† for decoration of the fcene. And they had the

42.
The Court
Mafques in
Jac. and
Car. I.
Operas.

---

* The Mafques of this period were court entertainments, or performed in the houfes of the nobility, on particular occafions of feftivity ; the neceffary machinery and decorations-rendered fuch exhibitions too expenfive for the ordinary public theatres. Indeed, the feveral parts in the Mafques of the fixteenth and feventeenth centuries were ufually reprefented by the firft perfonages in the kingdom ; if at court, the king, queen, and princes of the blood often performed in them. And this was the cuftom in France and other parts of Europe. The Mafques of James's Court were the precurfors of the Opera in England, and belong " to the chain of dramas which completed the union of poetry and mufic on our ftage." They were fpoken in dialogue, fometimes in recitative, performed on a ftage, ornamented by machinery, dreffes and decorations, and have always mufic both vocal and inftrumental. The chief writers of thefe entertainments were Ben Jonfon, John Daniel, and Dr. Campion. The compofers were Alfonfo Ferabofco, Nicholas Laniere, Thomas Lupo, Nathaniel Giles, and Dr. Campion the poet.

† A cuftom practifed in the early days of the mufical drama in Italy.

favour to be made a corporation,* with a charter, whereby they had divers priviledges, and a jurifdiction over the faculty, no lefs formal than the Colledge of Phifitians; and this charter is ftill in force, but not, as I know, made ufe of.† The mufick at thefe mafques (as muft be fuppofed),

---

* James I. in the fecond year of his reign, by letters patent incorporated the Muficians of the City of London into a COMPANY, and they ftill continue to enjoy privileges in confequence of their conftituting a fraternity and corporation; bearing arms azure, a fwan argent within a treffure counter-flure, or: in a chief, gules, a rofe between two lions, or: and for their creft the celeftial fign Lyra, called by aftronomers the Orphean Lyre. See Butler's *Principles of Mufick*, 1636, dedication; Playford's *Introduction to the fkill of Mufick*, edit. 1670; and Hatton's *New View of London*, 1708, ii. 612. Thomas Ravenfcroft (*Briefe Difcourfe*, 1614), fpeaks in no very favourable terms of this Company. (See Preface, fig. A. i.) Burney (*Hift. of Mufic*, iii. 359) fays that " this Company has ever been held in derifion by real profeffors, who have regarded it as an inftitution as foreign to the cultivation and profperity of good Mufic, as the train-bands to the art of war."

† The Company of Muficians, for a confiderable time after North wrote, continued to exclude from performances within the city fuch muficians as were not free of the Company. A remarkable inftance of this kind occurred in the year 1737. " One Povey, a whimfical man, and known to the world by his having been the original projector of the Penny-poft Office, engaged a number of muficians, fome from the opera, to play at a weekly concert, for which he obtained fubfcriptions, to be held in a great room in an old houfe in a court in St. Martin's le Grand. The firft night of performance was the Saturday after the interment of Queen Caroline; the bills and advertifements announced that an oration would be delivered, deploring the death of that princefs; but in the midft of the performance, fuch of the muficians as were known to be foreigners, were arrefted at the fuit of the Company of Muficians of London: a proceeding which, had it been contefted, would fcarcely have been warranted, feeing that St. Martin's le Grand is not part of the City of London, but a liberty of Weftminfter." (MS. note in the Editor's copy of Burney's *Hift. of Mufic*.)

was of the ayery kind,* with as much variety and novelty
as could be contrived to pleas the Court, and among other
conceipts there was a confort of 12 lutes, which muſt needs
be (in our dialeƈt) very fine and pretty. The entertainments
confifted of conforts, finging, machines, ſhort dramas, familiar dialogues, Interludes and dancing; wherein the yonger
quallity had no fmall ſhare. And taking the whole together,
and excepting the advantage of a fingle voice or two, thefe
diverſions were not inferior to our operas, and confidering
that the moſt vulgar compofition in a ſtately theater, comes
not ſhort of that which is more artfull, for magnitude and
force of found is among the cheif excellencys of muſick, provided there is in it no abſurdity. Wee muſt not brave it as
fome doe that there never was good muſick in England but
in our time.

It imparts not much to the ſtate of the world, or the condition of humane life, to know the names and ſtyles of thofe
authors of muficall compofition whofe performances gained
to the nation the credit of excelling the Itallians in all but
the vocall; therefore the oblivion that is come over all is no
great lofs. But for curiofity, as other no lefs idle antiquitys

* Specimens of the Court Mafque Mufic may be feen in *Ayres by Alfonfo
Ferrabofco*, 1609; *The Defcription of a Maſke prefented before the Kinges
Majeftie at White-Hall on Twelfth Night laſt, in honour of the Lord Hayes
and his Bride*, 1607; *Ayres made by Severall Authors and fung in the Maſke
at the Marriage of the Right Hon. Robert Earle of Somerfet and the Right
Noble Lady Frances Howard*, 1614; and *The Maſke of Flowers prefented by
the Gentlemen of Graies-Inne at the Court of Whitehall*, 1613.

are courted, any profeffor would be contented to know their names, and the caraƈters and works. And much might be done that way, if there were means to come at fome gentlemens old colleƈtions, not yet rotten, where many of them are ftill delitefcent, and there one might find fome of Alfonfo Ferabofco,* Coperario,† (anglice Cooper) Lupo,‡ Mico,§

---

 * Alfonfo Ferrabofco was born at Greenwich of Italian parents, about the year 1580. He was an intimate friend of Ben Jonfon, and compofed the mufic to many of his Mafques. In 1609 he publifhed two works, the *Ayres* (before noticed) and a colleƈtion of *Leffons for 1, 2, and 3 Viols.* Ben Jonfon wrote fome complimentary verfes on both occafions. He was living in 1641 when his name occurs in a warrant exempting the King's Muficians from the payment of fubfidies; Chriftopher Simpfon, (*Compendium of Praƈticall Mufick*) fpeaks of him as "deceafed" before the year 1665.

 † Giovanni Coperario was an Englifh mufician named John Cooper, who, after having fpent fome time in Italy, returned to his native country with an Italian cognomen. He compofed the mufic for the *Mafque of the Inner Temple and Gray's Inn,* 1612; and the *Mafke of Flowers,* 1614. He alfo affifted Laniere in compofing the mufic for the *Mafke prefented at the Marriage of the Earl of Somerfet and Lady Frances Howard,* 1614. He was a celebrated performer on the Lute and Viol da Gamba, and was the mufical inftruƈtor of the children of James I. In 1606 he publifhed *Funeral Teares for the death of the Right Hon. the Earle of Devonfhire, figured in Seaven Songs;* and in 1613, *Songs of Mourning bewailing the untimely death of Prince Henry.* He compofed a fet of Fancies for his royal pupil King Charles I. the original MS. of which is ftill extant. John Playford, fpeaking of Charles's fkill in mufic, fays, "He could play his part exaƈtly well on the Bafs-Viol, efpecially of thefe incomparable Fancies of Mr. Coperario to the Organ." (*Introduƈtion to the fkill of Mufick, edit.* 1683, Preface.) He died during the Proteƈtorate.

 ‡ Thomas Lupo was one of the Court Muficians to James I., and retained by Charles I. (See Rymer's *Fœdera,* xviii. 728.) He was appointed one of the muficians to Prince Henry at a falary of £40 yearly. (See Birch's *Life of Prince Henry.*) He compofed, in conjunƈtion with Thomas Giles and Dr.

Eft,* and divers others, efpecially of one Mr. John Jenkins, whofe muficall works are more voluminous, and in the time more efteemed then all the reft, and now lye in the utmoft contempt. I fhall adventure to give a fhort account of this particular mafter, with whom it was my good chance to have had an intimate acquaintance and friendfhip. He lived in King James' time,† and flourifhed in King Charles the firfts. His talents lay in the ufe of the Lute, and Bafe or rather Lyra-Viol;‡ he was one of the court mufitians, and once was brought to play upon the Lyra-Violl afore King Charles the firft, as one that performed fomewhat extraordinary. And after he had done, the King fayd he did wonders upon an inconfiderable inftrument. After the court was difbanded he

---

Campion, the mufic to a *Mafke in honour of Lord Hayes and his Bride*, performed at Whitehall in 1607. He died before the Reftoration.

§ A compofer of this name flourifhed in the reign of James and his fucceffor, but no particulars of him are known. Simpfon fpeaks of him as "deceafed" before the year 1665. (See Simpfon's *Compendium of Practicall Mufick*.)

* Michael Efte, Muf. Bac. and Mafter of the Chorifters of the Cathedral Church of Litchfield, was an eminent mufician of the feventeenth century. His vocal and inftrumental works are more numerous than many of his contemporaries, and confift of feven different collections of Madrigals, Part Songs, Anthems, and Fancies, all printed between the years 1600 and 1638. The dates of his birth and deceafe are uncertain.

† John Jenkins was born at Maidftone in Kent, in the year 1592. He ftudied mufic from childhood, and was greatly patronifed in early life by a Norfolk family of the name of Deerham.

‡ The Lyra-Viol was a Viol-da-Gamba, with fix ftrings, but differently tuned from the common fix-ftring bafs. Its notation like that of the lute was written in *entablature*. (See *Mufick's Recreation on the Lyra-Viol*, printed by John Playford, 1650.)

left the towne, and paffed his time at gentlemens houfes in the country, where mufick was of the family; and he was even courted and never flighted, but at home where ever he went. And in moft of his friends houfes there was a chamber called by his name, for befides his muficall excellencies he was an accomplifht ingenious perfon, and fo well behaved as never to give offence, and wherever he went was allwais welcome and courted to ftay. Even in his extream old age, when as to mufick he was almoft *effete*, and withall obnoxious to great infirmitys, he was taken care of as a friend, and after having fpent fome of the laft years of his life with Sir P. Woodehous,* he dyed at Kimberly† in Norfolk, and not

---

* " Sir Phillip Wodehoufe, Bart. was one of the burgeffes for Thetford, in that Parliament that reftored Charles II. A. D. 1660; he was baptized at Kimberley, July 24, 1608, and was a man of good learning, ready wit, and exceeding fkilful in mufick. He died at Kimberley, and was buried there May 6, 1681, of whom there is the following juft character on his grave-ftone, which hath the arms, creft, and motto of WODEHOUSE, impaling COTTON, *viz.* an eagle difplayed *or*, armed and beaked *gul.* and lies in the altar rails on the fouth fide :

Hic jacet PHILIPPUS WODEHOUSE, Bart. Qui in Deum,
Principem, et Patriam, Eximium Pietatis Exemplar emicuit,
Clementia fuit in fuos, omnefque quibufcam vixerat admiranda,
Theologiæ fimul et Philofophiæ ita operam dedit, ut utramque
Vita et Moribus expreflerit, Mufas et Muficam ftudiofe colens,
Vitam fibi et fuis amœniorem reddidit, Quumque Annos fere tres,
Supra Septuaginta exegerat, tranquillam obijt Mortem quinto
Nonas Maij, Anno Salutis 1681."

Blomefield's *Norfolk*, edit. 1805. ii. 556.

† The parifh regifter of Kimberly records that " John Jenkins, Efq." was " buried Oct. 29th 1678." In Blomefield's *Hift. of Norfolk*, vol. i. p. 759,

poor but capable to leave, as he did, hanfome remembrances to fome of his friends. I never heard that he articled with any gentleman where he refided, but accepted what they gave him. And he kept his places at Court, as I underftood to the time of his death, and then he for many years was uncapable to attend; the court mufitians had fo much value for him that advantage was not taken; but he received his falary as they were payd.

It is not poffible to give an account of his compofitions,* they were fo many that he himfelf outlived the knowledge of them. A fpanifh Don fent fome papers to Sir P. Lely,

44.
Of his com-
pofitions,
new, ayery,
and eafy.

the following epitaph is inferted, which is faid to have been copied from his grave-ftone in the middle of that church; but it is now gone.

> " Under this Stone rare *Jenkyns* lye,
>   The Mafter of the Mufick Art,
> Whom from the Earth, the God on high,
>   Called up to him, to bear his part.
> Aged 86, October 27,
> In Anno 78, he went to Heaven."

Anthony Wood (*Diary* Oxf. p. 94.) calls Jenkins " the mirrour and won-der of his age for Mufic." He was " excellent for the Lyra-Viol and Divifion-Viol, good at the Treble-Viol and Treble-Violin, and all comprehended in a man of three or 4 and twentie yeares of age. He was much admired at the [Oxford] Meetings, and exceedingly pittied by all the faculty for his lofs." In another place, he fays that Jenkins " though a little man, yet he had a great foul."

* In the library of the Mufic-School, Oxford, is preferved the following collection of Jenkins' Compofitions. 1. Fancies for Inftruments in fix parts to the organ; 2. Fancies for treble and two baffes to the organ (dated 1654);

conteining one part of a confort of 4., of a fprightly moving kind, fuch as were called Fancys, defiring that he would procure and fend him the other parts *cofta che cofta*. Lely gave me thefe papers, as the likelyeft perfon to get them fupplyed; I fhewed them to Jenkins, who fayd he knew the confort to be his, but when, or where made he knew not, and could not recollect any thing more concerning them. It is fuppofed that when he firft began to compofe, he followed in the track of the moft celebrated mafters, of whom I have named fome, and confequently his ftyle was, as theirs, folemne and grave. I have feen an *In nomine* of his of fix parts, moft elaborate; but his Lute and Lyra-Violl wrought fo much upon his fancy, that he diverted to a more lively ayre and was not onely an innovator, but became a reformer of mufick. His Fancys were full of ayery points, graves, tripla's, and other variety, and his leffer peices imitated the dulcer of Lute-leffons, of which he compofed multitudes; and all that he did, untill his declyning age, was lively, decided, and (if I may be credited) cappricciofo. And of this kind there was horfloads of his works, which were difperfed about, and very few came together into the fame hands; but the private

---

3. Fancies of four parts; 5. Fancies of three parts, 2nd fet; 6. Fancies of three parts to the organ; 7. Fancies of three parts to the organ, 2nd fet; 8. Ayres for two trebles and two baffes to the organ; 9. Ayres of four parts. In 1660, he publifhed *Twelve Sonatas for two Violins and a Bafe, with a Thorough Bafe for the Organ or Theorbo.* This work was reprinted at Amfterdam in 1664. None of the infinite number of pieces that he compofed for Viols, which occur in all the manufcript collections of the times, were printed. Jenkins's Sonatas were profeffedly in imitation of the Italian ftyle, and the firft of the kind which had ever been produced by an Englifhman.

muſick in England was, in great meaſure, ſupplyed by him; and they were courted becaus his ſtyle was new, and (for the time) difficult, for he could hardly forbear diviſions, and ſome of his conſorts was too full of them. And if that, as the moderne caprice will have it, be a recomendation, his compoſitions wanted it not; but this is further to be ſayd of him, that being an accompliſht maſter of the viol, all his movements lay fair for the hand and were not ſo hard as ſeemed.

His vein was leſs happy in the vocall part, for tho' he took pleaſure in putting muſick to poems,* he reteined his inſtrumentall ſtyle ſo much, that few of them were greatly approved. Nor was his teaching ſcollars to ſing (as for want of profeſſed maſters he did) better, for he had neither a voice, nor any manner fitt for it. But ſome anthems of his remain

45.
Fell ſhort in the vocall; ſome pieces humourſome.

---

* In 1652 was publiſhed a work entitled *Theophila or Love's Sacrifice, a Divine Poem by E(dward) B(enlowe) Eſq. ſeveral parts thereof ſet to fit aires by Mr. J. Jenkins.* He alſo wrote " An Elegiack Dialogue on the ſad loſſe of his much admired friend Mr. William Lawes, Servant to his Majeſtie," printed in the *Choice Pſalmes put into Muſick for three Voices. Compoſed by Henry and William Lawes.* 1648. The other publiſhed vocal compoſitions of this author are the following : " A boat, a boat," and " Come pretty maidens," two rounds, printed in John Hilton's *Catch that catch can,* 1652 ; " See ſee the bright light," a ſong for two voices, printed in the *Treaſury of Muſick,* Bk. i. 1669 ; " Why ſighs thou Shepherd ?" a dialogue and chorus, alſo inſerted in the ſame work, and " When fair Aurora," a ſong for two voices, printed in the ſecond part of the *Muſical Companion,* 1672. The words of an " Hymn on the Divine uſe of Muſick," beginning " We ſing to him whoſe wiſdom form'd the ear," are prefixed to Playford's *Pſalmes and Hymns,* 1671, and ſaid to be " Compoſed to Muſick for three Voyces by Mr. John Jenkins."

in the Cathedralls, where they are in cours fung, and, in that fervice, are not amifs. He would be often in a merry humour, and make Catches, and fome ftrains he called Rants,* which were like our ftaccatas. He made a peice called the *Cryes of Newgate*, which was all humour, and very bizzarre. But of all his conceipts, none flew about with his name fo univerfally as the fmall peice called his *Bells*.† In thofe days the country fidlers were not fo well foddered from London, as fince, and a mafter that made new tunes for them, was a benefactor. And thefe *Bells* was fuch fupply, as never failed to pafs in all companys. It was a happy thought, and well

---

* " The Mitter Rant," compofed by John Jenkins, was a favourite tune in the latter part of the feventeenth century. It may be feen in Playford's *Mufick's Hand-maid*, 1678, and many other publications of the time. " The Fleece Tavern Rant," and " The Peterborough Rant," two popular airs of the time, were alfo the compofition of Jenkins. See Playford's *Apollo's Banquet*. 1690.

† Dr. Burney (*Hift. of Mufic*, iii. 413) fays, " What gave rife to this Trio or *Confort*, as it was called, feems to have been a book called *Tintinalogia, or the Art of Ringing*, publifhed in 1668 ; a work not beneath the notice of muficians who wifh to explore all the regions of natural melody." Dr. Bufby (*Hift. of Mufic*, ii. 189) fays, " *About* the year 1668, a book entitled *Tintinalogia*, &c. was publifhed. It excited very general attention ; and Jenkins, having perufed the contents, was ftruck with the idea of compofing a piece analogous to the mufic of the bells." Unfortunately however for the theory of the two Doctors, Jenkins' " Five bell Conforte" was compofed and publifhed *fix* years before the appearance of the faid work on the art of ringing. This " Conforte" was compofed at the requeft of Lady Katherine Audley, who had refided in the Netherlands, and had imbibed a love for Carillions, and was named after her, " The Lady Katherine Audley's Bells, or the Five Bell Conforte." It was firft printed in John Playford's *Courtly Mafquing Ayres*, 1662, but in *two* parts only. The *third* part (as given by Burney) was added by the Compofer at a fubfequent period.

executed, and for the variety, might be ftyled a Sonnata;
onely the found of bells being among the vulgaritys, tho'
naturally elegant enough, like comon fweetmeats, grows ful-
fome, and will not be endured longer then the humour of
affecting a novelty lafts.

It will be now afked how it can confift that the mufick of
Mr. Jenkins, if it were fuch as here is pretended, fhould be
now fo much layd afide, or rather contemned as it is, when
the art is thought to be arrived at a perfection. This would
be harder to anfwer, if it were not a great truth, and notori-
ous, that every age fince Apollo did not fay the fame thing
of the mufick of their owne time. For nothing is more a
fafhion then mufick; no not cloathes, or language, either of
which is made a derifion to after times. And fo it is of all
things that belong to the pleafures of fence. For allowing
that there is fomewhat preferable in right reafon, as fome
cloathes may be more convenient, and language concife, and
fignificant; yet there is a great deal indifferent, and fo much,
that the prejudice of cuftome will get the better of it. And the
grand cuftome of all is to affect novelty, and to goe from one
thing to another, and defpife the former. And it is a poor-
nefs of fpirit, and a low method of thinking, that inclines
men to pronounce for the prefent, and allow nothing to times
paft. Cannot wee put ourfelves in *loco* of former ftates, and
judge *pro tunc ?* Therefore as to all *bon gufto* wee ought to
yield to the authority of the proper time, and not determine
comparatively where one fide is all prejudice. It is a fhallow
monfter that fhall hold forth in favour of our fafhions and

46.
Why now
layd afide.

relifhes, and maintaine that no age fhall come wherein they will not be defpifed and derided. And if on the other fide, I may take upon me to be a fidling prophet, I may with as much reafon declare that the time may come when fome of the prefent celebrated mufick will be as much in contempt as *John com kifs me now, now, now,** and perhaps with as much reafon, as any is found for the contrary at prefent.

---

* The air of " John come kifs me now," corrupted from " *Joan* come kifs me now," was once a popular theme for fancies and divifions, for the Virginals, Lute, and Viol. It may be feen, with variations for the Virginals by William Byrd, in Queen Elizabeth's Virginal Book; and with variations for the Violin by David Mell, and Thomas Baltzar, in Playford's *Divifion Violin*, 1685. The words of this popular ballad were paraphrafed in *Ane Compendious Booke of Godly and Spirituall Songs*, Edinb. 1590.

The monftrous effect of the *feria mifta jocis*, in matters of a religious nature, has feldom been fo glaringly exemplified as in fome of the " godly and fpiritual fongs" as they were ftrangely mifcalled, to be found in this *Compendium*. " John come kifs me now," as Mr. Tytler well obferves, " makes his appearance, ftripped, indeed, of his profane drefs, which had promoted ' fin and harlotrie,' but in exchange, fo ftrangely equipped in his penitential habit, as to make a more ludicrous figure than his brother Jack in the *Tale of a Tub*."

" Johne, cum kis me now,
    Johne, cum kis me now;
Johne, cum kis me by and by,
    And make no more adow.

The Lord thy God I am,
    That John dois thee call
John reprefents man,
    By grace celeftiall

My prophites call, my preachers cry,
    Johne, cum kis me now;
Johne, cum kis me by and by,
    And make no more adow."

But as to Mr. Jenkins in particular, there is fomewhat more to be fayd; his ftyle is thought to be flow, heavy, moving from concord to concord, & confequently dull. And I grant that he was obnoxious to an excefs the englifh were, and I believe yet are, obnoxious too—and that is perpetually moving up and downe, without much faltation or battering as the Italians ufe. But els as to activity of movement, and true muficall ayre in his paffages, none had more than Mr. Jenkins; but the unhappynes is that all his earlyeft and moft lively compofitions are funk and loft, and none remaine but thofe of his latter time, when he lived in country family's, and could compofe no otherwife then to the capacity of his performers, who could not deal with his high flying vein. It is no wonder that few or none but thofe of the latter fort are to be met with; and fo the whole force of a man is meafured according to a member that is lamed. But in his old age he made fome effays of his art which, not being ufeful where he refided, I had the honour to carry as a prefent from him to good Mr. Stephkins,* who was much efteemed by him; whither they are extant or not I know not. He was certeinly a great mafter of divifions, and encouraged

---

The popularity of this air at various periods is evinced by the notices of it in Heywood's *Woman killed with kindnefs*, 1600; *Tis merry when Goffips meet*, 1609; Burton's *Anatomy of Melancholy*, 1621; *Weftminfter Drollery*, 1671; Henry Bold's *Songs and Poems*, 1685, &c.

* Theodorus Stefkins was a foreign profeffor of the Viol, refident in London in the latter half of the feventeenth century. He is fpoken of with commendation in Salmon's *Effay to the Advancement of Mufick*, &c. 1672, p. 82. Frederick and Chriftian, his two fons, were alfo famous performers on the Viol,

Sympſon, the Diviſion Violiſt, by a copy of verſes at the beginning, and ſome examplars of diviſions at the latter end of
his book.* But as plaine as his latter compoſitions are, if
performed (not with dull but) briſk hands, diſtinguiſhing the
graves and allegro's, I may challenge the moſt ſkillfull of the
maſters (faſhion apart) to find fault with the muſick; for his
ayre is unexceptionable, and if he hath not ſo many hard
notes as are now uſed, (which by the way are not abſolutely
neceſſary, but onely as an ornament to harmony) a ſkillful
hand will ſupply enough of them, for there are very few but
what occur in the comon gracing of muſicall performances.
And now to conclude as to Mr. Jenkins, he was certeinly
a very happy perſon, for he had an uninterupted health and
was of an eaſy temper, ſuperior in his profeſſion, well accepted
by all, knew no want, ſaw himſelf outrun by the world, and
having lived a good chriſtian, dyed in peace.

(See *The Theory of Muſic reduced to arithmetical and geometrical proportions*, by
Thomas Salmon, printed in the *Philoſophical Tranſactions of the Royal Society*,
Jones's *Abridg.* vol. iv. pt. 11. p. 469.) They were members of the royal band
of King William in 1694 (See Chamberlayne's *Preſent ſtate of England*, printed
in that year). The elder Stefkins had a brother named "Deitricht" who was
one of the royal band of Charles the Firſt in 1641 (See Collier's *Annals of the
Stage*, vol. ii. p. 103).

* Chriſtopher Simpſon's *Compendium of Practical Muſick* was deſervedly
popular for more than half a century after its firſt appearance. The *firſt* edition
was printed in 1665 (not 1666, as generally ſtated); the *ſecond* in 1667; the
third in 1678; the *fourth* in 1706; the *fifth* in 1714; the *ſixth* in 1721; the
ſeventh in 1727; the *eighth* in 1732; and the *ninth* and laſt (publiſhed without
date) about 1790. Jenkins addreſſes Simpſon as "his much Honoured and
very precious Friend." The "examplars of diviſions" were firſt prefixed to
the third edition of the work.

Mr. Math. Lock was the moſt conſiderable maſter of muſick after Jenkins fell off.* He was organiſt at Somerſet
hous chappell as long as he lived,† but the Itallian maſters,
that ſerved there, did not approve of his manner of play, but
muſt be attended by more polite hands ; and one while one
Sabinico,‡ and afterwards Sig. Baptiſta Draghi§ uſed the

48.
Mr. M.
Lock a good
Compoſer in
the old and
new way.

---

* Matthew Lock was a native of Exeter, and a choriſter in the Cathedral of
that city, where he was initiated in muſic by William Wake, the organiſt. He
afterwards received inſtruction from Edward Gibbons, the organiſt of Briſtol
Cathedral, and very early in life attained a conſiderable degree of eminence in
his profeſſion. We learn from Ogilby's *Relation of His Majeſty's Entertainment paſſing through the City of London to his Coronation*, April 22, 1661, that
he compoſed the whole of the muſic for the public entry of Charles II. ; on
which occaſion he received the appointment of " Compoſer in Ordinary" to
that monarch.

† It is preſumed that when Lock was appointed Compoſer in Ordinary to the
King, he was profeſſedly a member of the Church of England ; but towards
the latter part of his life he became a Roman Catholic, and was appointed Organiſt to Queen Catherine of Portugal, the conſort of Charles II. The Queen
was permitted the exerciſe of her religion, and had a chapel at Somerſet-houſe,
(the palace of the Queen Dowager,) together with a regular eccleſiaſtical eſta-
bliſhment. It ſeems probable that Lock alſo reſided in the palace, for his laſt
publication is dated from his lodgings in the Strand. He died in 1677, and was
buried in the Savoy. The celebrated Henry Purcell wrote an elegy " On the
Death of his Worthy Friend Mr. Matthew Locke, Muſick-compoſer in Ordinary to his Majeſty, and Organiſt of her Majeſties Chappell, who dyed in
Auguſt 1677." It is printed in the ſecond book of the *Choice Ayres and Dialogues*, 1679.

‡ An obſcure Italian muſician who came to this country with Mary D'Eſte,
princeſs of Modena. Some of his compoſitions are preſerved in the Oxford
Muſick School.

§ Giovanni Battiſta Draghi was an Italian by birth, and probably related to
Antonio Draghi, Maeſtro di Capella at Vienna, and Carlo Draghi, organiſt to

great organ, and Lock (who muſt not be turned out of his place, nor the execution) had a ſmall chamber organ by, on which he performed with them the ſame ſervices. In muſick he had a robuſt vein, and many of his compoſitions went about; he ſet moſt of the pſalmes to muſick in parts, for the uſe of ſome vertuoſo ladyes in the city; * and he compoſed a magnifick conſort of 4 parts after the old ſtyle,† which was the laſt of the kind that hath been made, ſo wee may rank him with Cleomenes King of Sparta, who was ſtyled *ultimus herooum*. He conformed at laſt to the modes of his time, and fell into the theatricall way, and compoſed to the ſemioperas divers peices of vocall and inſtrumentall entertainment, with very good ſucceſs;‡ and then gave way to the divine Purcell

---

the Emperor Leopold. He was an excellent compoſer, and joined with Lock in compoſing the muſic to Shadwell's Opera of Pſyche, produced in 1673.

   * The original MS. of the Pſalms compoſed by Lock for " the vertuoſo ladyes in the city" is now in the Editor's library. It was formerly in the poſſeſſion of Dr. W. Hayes. It is written in a ſmall neat hand on forty-nine folio pages, and contains the following anthems (the words ſelected from the Pſalms), for three and four voices :—Bleſſed is the man ; O Lord, rebuke me not ; O Lord, how marvellous ; Let God ariſe ; Behold, how good and joyful ; Praiſe the Lord, all ye Gentiles ; When I was in tribulation ; Sing unto the Lord ; From the depths ; O Lord, hear my prayer ; In the beginning, O Lord ; Ariſe O Lord ; Lord, now letteſt thou. At the end are ſeveral latin hymns for voices and inſtruments, probably compoſed for the Chapel of Queen Catherine. A large number of Lock's ſacred compoſitions are preſerved in the Fitzwilliam Muſeum, and in the library of Ely Cathedral.

   † In Bartleman's Sale Catalogue, lot 101 is thus deſcribed : " Locke (M) Concert of 4 parts *ſcored by his own hand.*" See alſo the ſale catalogue of Edward Jones, the Welſh bard. (Lot. 476.)

   ‡ Lock's firſt attempt at dramatic compoſition was probably Shirley's maſque

and others, that were coming full fail into the fuperiority of the muficall faculty.

But now to obferve the ftepps of the grand metamorfofis of mufick, whereby it hath mounted into thofe altitudes of efteem it now enjoys. I muft remember that upon the reftauration of King Charles, the old way of conforts were layd afide at court, and the King made an eftablifhment, after a french model, of 24 violins,* & the ftyle of the mufick was

49.
The band of violins, Mr. Baltefar, and the ftyle of Baptift.

---

of *Cupid and Death* performed in 1653. A complete copy, in the hand writing of the compofer, is ftill extant (See Dr. Rimbault's Preface to *Bonduca*, publifhed by the Mufical Antiquarian Society, p. 13). He alfo compofed the mufic for *The Step Mother*, 1663; *The Tempeft*, 1670; *Pfyche*, 1673, and probably many other pieces not recorded. The mufic of Macbeth, now popularly known as Lock's, is the compofition of Richard Leveridge and was performed for the firft time on the 25th January, 1704. Lock's mufic compofed in the reign of Charles II. is entirely different.

* It was not until the reftoration of Charles II. that inftruments of the violin fpecies formed the exclufive royal band. The ftate band of Henry VIII. (1526) confifted of 15 trumpets, 3 lutes, 3 rebecks, 3 taborets, a harp, 2 viols, 4 drumflades, a fife, and 10 fackbuts.—(MS. roll in the Editor's poffeffion.) The firft mention of violins in the royal band occurs in the year 1561 (4th Eliz.), when the annual amount paid to the performers on that inftrument amounted to 230*l*. 6*s*. 8*d*. (See MS. *Lanfd.* No. 5.) In 1571 the coft was confiderably increafed, as we learn by the following entry in the royal book of expenditure for that year (MS. *Cott. Vefp.* C. xiv.):—" Item to the vyolons, being vij of them, every one at 20*d*. per diem for their wages, and 16*l*. 2*s*. 6*d*. for their lyveries. In all per ann. 325*l*. 15*s*. 0*d*." The royal band of Charles I. (1625) confifted of 8 hautboys and fackbuts, 6 flutes, 6 recorders, 11 *violins*, 6 lutes, 4 viols and a harp, exclufive of trumpeters, drummers, and fifers. By a warrant in the Rolls houfe, dated April 17, 1641, exempting the king's fervants from the payment of fubfidies, we learn that the royal band then confifted of no lefs than fifty-eight muficians. The violin was now rapidly rifing

accordingly. So that became the ordinary mufick of the court, theatres, and fuch as courted the violin. And that

in eftimation, and the following lift of performers (included in the warrant juft noticed) contains the names of feveral afterwards highly diftinguifhed in their profeffion.

"*Muficians for the Violins.*

Thomas Lupo	Nicholas Pikard	Ambrofe Byland
Thomas Warren	Stephen Nau	Theophilus Lupo
Leonard Mell	Richard Dorney	Baftien Lapiere
John Hopper	James Woodington	George Turgis."
Davies Mell	Simon Nau	

Charles II. who during the ufurpation had fpent a confiderable time on the continent, where he heard nothing but French mufic, upon his return to England, in imitation of Louis XIV., eftablifhed a band of violins, tenors, and baffes, commonly known as the four-and-twenty fiddlers. Anthony Wood (*Account of his Life*, p. 97), fpeaking of the introduction of the violin into the Oxford mufic meetings, fays: "but before the Reftoration of K. Ch. 2. and efpecially after, Viols began to be out of fafhion, and only Violins ufed, as Treble-Violin, Tenor, and Bafs-Violin; and the King, according to the French mode, would have 24 Violins playing before him, while he was at meales, as being more airie and brifk than Viols." It would have been well had the King confined the performance of his "four-and-twenty fiddlers" to the accompaniment of his "meales." John Evelyn fpeaking of a vifit to the royal chapel (Dec. 21, 1662, *Diary*, vol. i. p. 356), fays "One of his Majefties chaplains preach'd, after which, inftead of the antient, grave, and folemn wind mufiq accompanying the organ, was introduced a concert of 24 violins betweene every paufe, after the French fantaftical light way, better fuiting a tavern or playhoufe than a church." An exchequer document, in the editor's poffeffion, contains the names of the royal "twenty-four" with the amounts of their refpective falaries. The document runs thus.

"The Names of the Gents of his Majefties Private Mufick paid out of the Excheker.

	£.	s.	d.
Tho. Purcell . . . . . ⎫			
Pelham Humpreys . . . . ⎭	200	0	0

inftrument had a lift into credit before, for one Baltzar,* a Swede, came over and did wonders upon it by fwiftnefs and

John Hardinge	.	.	.	.	.	40	0	0
William Hawes	.	.	.	.	.	46	10	10
Tho. Blagrave, *fen.*		.	.	.	.	40	9	2
Alf. Marfh	.	.	.	.	.	40	0	0
John Goodgroome	.	.	.	.	.	40	0	0
Nat. Wattkins	.	.	.	.	.	40	0	0
Mat. Lock	.	.	.	.	.	40	0	0
John Clayton	.	.	.	.	.	152	13	4
Izaack Stagins, *fen.*		.	.	.	.	46	10	10
Nich. Stagins, *jun.*		.	.	.	.	46	10	10
Tho. Battes	.	.	.	.	.	90	0	0
John Lilly	.	.	.	.	.	40	0	0
Hen. Gregory	.	.	.	.	.	60	0	0
Theop. Hills	.	.	.	.	.	46	10	10
Hen. Madge	.	.	.	.	.	86	12	8
John Gambell	.	.	.	.	.	46	10	10
Rich. Dorney	.	.	.	.	.	20	0	0
John Banifter, *fen.*	.	.	.	.	.	100	0	0
Phil. Beckett	.	.	.	.	.	60	2	6
Rob. Blagrave, *jun.*		.	.	.	.	58	4	2
John Singleton	.	.	.	.	.	46	10	10
Rob. Strange	.	.	.	.	.	46	10	10

15 May, 1674. (Signed) T. Purcell."

* Thomas Baltzar, born at Lubeck, about 1630, was efteemed the fineft performer on the violin of his time. He came to England in 1656 (not 1658, as generally ftated), at which time the inftrument had not yet been enabled to affert its powers here, nor to emerge (as it fhortly afterwards did), from the low eftimation in which it was held. An account of Baltzar's performance fhortly after his arrival here, has been left us by John Evelyn. Under the date of March 4, 1656 (*Diary*, vol. i. p. 298), that amufing writer tells us, " This night I was invited by Mr. Roger L'Eftrange to hear the incomparable Lubicer on the Violin. His variety on a few notes and plaine ground with that wonderful dexterity was admirable. Tho' a young man, yet fo perfect and fkillful

doubling of notes, but his hand was accounted hard and rough, tho' he made amends for that by ufing often a lyra-

---

that there was nothing, however crofs and perplext, brought to him by our Artifts, which he did not play off at fight with ravifhing fweetnefs and improvements, to the aftonifhment of our beft Mafters. In fum he plaid on that fingle inftrument a full concert, fo as the reft flung down their inftruments, acknowledging the victory. As to my own particular, I ftand to this hour amaz'd that God fhould give fo greate perfection to fo young a perfon. There were at that time as excellent in their profeffion as any were thought to be in Europe, Paul Wheeler, Mr. Mell, and others, till this prodigie appear'd. I can no longer queftion the effects we reade of in David's harp to charme evil fpirits, or what is faid fome particular notes produced in the paffions of Alexander, and that King of Denmark." Anthony Wood (*Diary of his Life*, 1772, p. 111) tells us, under the year 1658, that "Tho. Balfar, or Baltzar, a Lubecker borne, and the moft famous artift for the Violin that the world had yet produced was now in Oxon, and this day (July 24) A. W. (Anthony Wood) was with him and Mr. Edw. Low, lately Organift of Ch. Church, at the Meeting houfe of Will. Ellis. A. W. did then and there, to his very great aftonifhment, heare him play on the Violin. He then faw him run up his fingers to the end of the Finger-board of the violin, and run them back infenfibly, and all with alacrity and in very good tune, which he nor any in England faw the like before. A. W. entertain'd him and Mr. Low with what the houfe could then afford, and afterwards he invited them to the Tavern; but they being engaged to other company, he could no more heare him play or fee him play at that time. Afterwards he came to one of the weekly meetings at Mr. Ellis's houfe, and he played to the wonder of all the auditory: and exercifing his fingers and inftrument feveral wayes to the utmoft of his power, Wilfon thereupon the public Profeffor (the greateft judge of mufick that ever was) did after his humourfome way, ftoop downe to Baltzar's feet to fee whether he had a huff (hoof) on, that is to fay, to fee whether he was a devil or not, becaufe he acted beyond the parts of Man. About that time it was, that Dr. Joh. Wilkins, Warden of Wadham Coll. the greateft curiofo of his time, invited him and fome of the mufitians to his lodgings in that Coll. purpofely to have a Confort, and to fee and heare him play. The inftruments and books were carried thither, but none could be perfwaded there to play againft him in confort on the

tuning, and conformable leſſons, which were very harmonious, as coppys now extant in divers hands may ſhew ; but

---

violin.   At length the company perceiving A. W. ſtanding behind in a corner
neare the dore, they haled him in among them, and play, forſooth he muſt
againſt him.   Whereupon he being not able to avoid it, he took up a violin
and behaved himſelf as poor Troylus did againſt Achilles.   He was abaſhed at
it, yet honour he got by playing with and againſt ſuch a grand maſter as Baltzar was.   Mr. Davis Mell was accounted hithertoo the beſt for the Violin in
England, as I have before told you ; but after Baltzar came into England, and
ſhew'd his moſt wonderful parts on that inſtrument, Mell was not ſo admired,
yet he played ſweeter, was a well bred gentleman, and not given to exceſſive
drinking as Baltzar was."   At the reſtoration of Charles II. Baltzar was appointed leader of the King's band of twenty-four violins, and about the ſame
time, according to Wood, (*Lives of Engliſh Muſicians*, MS. in the Aſhmolean
Muſeum, No. 8568) " he commenced bachelar of muſick at Cambridge."
This celebrated violiniſt died in July 1663, and was buried in the cloiſter adjoining to Weſtminſter Abbey.   Wood (*Diary of his Life*, p. 190) ſays of him
that " being much admired by all lovers of muſick, his company was therefore
deſired : and company, eſpecially muſicall company, delighting in drinking,
made him drink more than ordinary, which brought him to his grave."
   The arrival of Baltzar in this country may be conſidered as an event which
tended in no ſmall degree to place the violin in that ſtation among the *ſtringed*
tribe which it has ſince ſo deſervedly occupied.   He is ſaid to have firſt taught
the Engliſh the practice of ſhifting (that is to ſay of what is termed the *whole-
ſhift*) and the uſe of the upper part of the finger-board.   It is certain that the
power of execution and command of the inſtrument exhibited by Baltzar were
matter of novelty among us, although we had a native performer of no mean
abilities at that period, in the perſon of Davis Mell, who in delicacy of tone and
manner, ſeems even to have exceeded the more potent and renowned German.
Dr. Burney, ſpeaking of Baltzar's merits as a compoſer, ſays, " his compoſitions
have more force and variety in them, and conſequently required more hand to
execute them, than any muſic then known for his inſtrument."
   The compoſitions of Baltzar are now very rarely met with.   Dr. Burney (*Hiſt.
of Muſic*, vol. iii. p. 428, *note*) mentions a MS. collection of his ſolos then in
his poſſeſſion, and which had been preſented to him by the Rev. Dr. Montague

this manner, which was but a complement to the lute, and
not fit for confort, did not take at all.   But during the firft
years of Charles the Second all mufick affected by the *beau
mond* run into the french way ; and the rather, becaus at that
time the mafter of the Court mufick in France, whofe name
was Baptifta,* (an Italian frenchifyed,) had influenced the
french ftyle by infufing a great portion of the Italian harmony into it, whereby the ayre was exceedingly improved.
The manner was theatricall, and the fetts of leffons compofed,
called Branles (as I take it), or Braules, that is beginning
with an Entry, and then Courant etc.† And the Entrys of
Baptift ever were, and will be valued as moft ftately and
compleat harmony ; and all the compofitions of the town
were ftrained to imitate Baptifts vein ; and none came fo neer

North. " A Set of Sonatas by Baltzar for a lyra violin, treble violin, and
bafs," formed lot 55 of the fale catalogue of Thomas Britton, the mufical
fmall-coal man.   The only *printed* compofitions of this mafter are the folos
contained in Henry Playford's *Divifion Violin*, 1692.

  * Jean Baptifte Lulli, the fon of a Tufcan peafant, born 1633, died 1687.
He contributed greatly to the improvement of inftrumental mufic, and invented
the dramatic overture.   Handel took him as a model for his opera-overtures.

  † The word *brawl* in its fignification of a dance is from the French *branle*,
indicating a fhaking or fwinging motion.   The mufic to a great variety of
brawls is given in the curious treatife on dancing by Thoinet Arbeau, entitled
Orchefographie, Lengres, 1588, 4to.   The *brawl* continued in fafhion until a
very late period both in England and France.   See Playford's publications, *The
Englifh Dancing Mafter ; Apollo's Banquet ; Treble-Violin Book ; Divifion
Violin*, &c.   At the end of the feventeenth century was publifhed " At the
mufick printer's next the Sun Tavern Holborn," *Leffons for the Harpfichord or
Spinet, viz. Almands, Corants, Sarabands, Airs, Minuets, Jiggs, Brawls, En-
tries, &c.   Compofed by Mr. Baptift Lully.*

it as the honorable and worthy vertuofo Mr. Francis Roberts.* But the whole tendency of the ayre had more regard to the foot, then the ear, and no one could hear an Entree with its ſtarts, and faults, but muſt expeᏛ a dance to follow, ſo lively may human aᏛions be piᏛured by muſick.

King Charles the Second was a profeſſed lover of muſick,† but of this kind onely, and had an utter deteſtation of Fancys, and the leſs for a ſucceſſleſs entertainment of that kind given him by Secretary Williamſon, after which the Secretary had no peace, for the King (as his way was) could not forbear whetting his wit upon the ſubjeᏛ of the fancy-muſick, and its patron the Secretary. And he would not allow the matter to be diſputed upon the point of meliority, but run all downe by ſaying, *Have not I ears?* He could not bear any muſick

50.
King Char.
2d. a novel-
liſt; and a
compariſon
of nations.

---

* The Hon. Francis Roberts was the author of a Paper on the Trumpet, and Trumpet Marine, printed in the Philoſophical TranſaᏛions for 1692. This Paper is alluded to in terms of praiſe, by Ambroſe Warren in a ſcarce traᏛ entitled *The Tonometer*, 1725, p. 8.

† Charles the Second had a ſlight knowledge of muſic; he underſtood the notes, and ſung, to uſe the expreſſion of one who had often ſung with him, " a plump baſs ;" but it nowhere appears that he conſidered muſic in any other view than as an incentive to mirth. In a letter of his to Henry Bennet, afterwards Earl of Arlington, dated from Bruges, Auguſt 18, 1655, he ſays, " Pray get me pricked down as many new Corrant and Sarrabands and other little dances as you can, and bring them with you, for I have got a ſmall fidler that does not play ill on the fiddle (ſee the *Account of the Preſervation of King Charles II.* &c. p. 150); and in another letter to the ſame perſon, dated Sept. 1, 1656, he ſays, " You will find by my laſt, that though I am furniſhed with one ſmall fidler, yet I would have another that plays well, I would have you do it." (*Ibid.* p. 168.)

to which he could not keep the time, and that he conftantly did to all that was prefented to him; and for the moft part heard it ftanding. And for fongs he approved onely the foft vein, fuch as might be called a ftep tripla,* and that made a fafhion among the mafters, and for the ftage, as may be feen in the printed books of the fongs of that time. Once the King had a fancy, for a comparifon, to hear the fingers of the feveral nations, Germans, Spanifh, Italian, French, and Eng-lifh, performe upon the ftage in Whitehall. The Itallians had that mentioned elfwhere, *Che dite, che fatti,* &c.† The Englifh brought up the arrere under great difadvantage, with *I pafs all my hours in a fhady old grove,* &c.‡ For the King chofe that fong as the beft; others were not of his opinion.

* The young chapel compofers, Humphries, Blow, and Wife, by the intro-duction of feveral of thefe movements, are accufed by Dr. Tudway, and others, of indulging the King's French tafte fo far as to introduce theatrical *corants* and dancing movements into their anthems. Even the great Purcell is not exempt from this charge, and many of his fineft anthems are disfigured by *fid-dling fymphonies* invented only to tickle the ears of the wretched Charles. They are now wifely left out in performance.

† Compofed by Giacomo Cariffimi, Chapel Mafter of the German College at Rome, about 1640. Purcell was much indebted to the productions of this great mafter. Dr. Aldrich formed a large Collection of his Cantatas, which is ftill preferved in the library of Chrift Church, Oxford.

‡ This fong, beginning,
> " I pafs all my hours in a fhady old grove,
> But I live not the day when I fee not my love ;
> I furvey ev'ry walk now my Phillis is gone,
> And figh when I think we were there all alone :
>> Oh then tis ! oh then ! that I think there's no Hell,
>> Like loving, like loving too well,"

was written by the King himfelf, and compofed by Pelham Humphries. It is

The French manner of Inftrumentall mufick did not gather fo faft as to make a revolution all at once, but during the greateft part of that king's reigne, the old mufick was ufed in the countrys, and in many meetings and focietys in London. But the treble-violl was difregarded, and the violin took its place. In fome familyes organs were ufed to accompany conforts, but the old mafters would not allow the liberty of playing from a thro' bafe figured, as harpfichords of late have univerfally practifed, but they formed the organ part exprefs; becaufe the holding out the found required exact concord, els the confort would fuffer; or perhaps the organifts had not then the fkill as fince, for now they defire onely figures. They were alfo divers Societys of a politer fort, who were inquifitive after forrein conforts, and procured divers, as from Itally, Cazzati,* & Vitali;† and one from Sweden by

51.
Old Mufick and forrein, retained by fome.

---

printed in *Choice Ayres, Songs, and Dialogues to fing to the Theorbo-Lute, or Bafs Viol; being moft of the Neweft Ayres and Songs, Sung at Court and at the Publick Theatres*, 1676. folio.

   * Mauritio Cazzati, born at Mantua, was, in the year 1664, Chapel Mafter to the Church of St. Peter at Bologna (See Mafini, *Bologna Perluftrata*, p. 687). The following works of this author are preferved in the Mufic School, Oxford: "Il fecondo libro delle Sonate a tre, due Violini, e' Violone, con il fue Baffo continuo. *Bologna.* 1648." "Canzonè da Sonare a tre, due Violini è Violone, con il fue Baffo continuo. *Bologna.* 1663." "Correnti e Balletti alla Francefe et all' Italiana. *Bologna.* 1667." Walther (*Muficalifches Lexicon*, p. 150) mentions feveral other works of this writer, whofe productions, inftrumental and vocal, in the year 1678, amounted to *fixty-five.*

   † Giovanni Battifta Vitali, a native of Cremona, publifhed many inftrumental works at the latter end of the feventeenth century. They are not recorded by Walther. The Oxford Mufic School contains the following:

Becker,* compofed for from 2 to 6 parts, which was too good
to be neglected and loft, as it is at prefent. And however
England came to have the credit of muficall lovers, I know
not, but am fure that there was a great flocking hither of
forrein mafters, as from Germany, Sheiffar,† Voglefank,‡
and others; and from France, Porter§ and Farinell,‖ thefe
latter for the violin. And they found here good encouragement, fo that the nation, (as I may term it) of mufick was
very well prepared for a revolution.

"Varie Sonate alla Francefe et all' Itagliana à fei Stromenti. *Modena*. 1684."
"Sonate a due Violini. *Venetia*, 1685." "Balleti a due Violini. *Venetia*,
1685." "Correnti e Balleti da Camera a due Violini, col fuo Baffo continuo
per Spinetta o' Violone *Bologna*, 1686." "Sonate a tre, doi Violini, e violon-
cello col Baffo per l' Organo. *Modena*. 1693."

* Dietrich Becker, one of the ftate violin players at Hamburgh, publifhed
Sonatas for a Violin, Viol da Gamba, and Baffo continuo, in 1668 (See Walther, *Muficalifches Lexicon*, p. 82). Dr. Burney (*Hift. of Mufic*, vol. iv. p.
579) fays "The violin fonatas of Becker were well known in England during
the latter end of the laft century, and I have copies of many of them, but they
are of a coarfe texture." Henry Playford in his "General Catalogue of all the
Choiceft Mufick-books" (Harl. MS. No. 5936) advertifes "Beccar's Sonatas
in 5 parts."

† This compofer's name does not occur in any biographical or bibliographical
work that the editor has confulted.

‡ Johann Vogelfank, a native of Lindau; the grandfon of the celebrated
theorift of the fame name. His works are but little known.

§ Ercole Porta, a celebrated Bolognefe compofer of inftrumental mufic in
the latter half of the feventeenth century. He publifhed a fet of Sonatas at
Paris in 1675.

‖ Farinelli, compofer, violinift and director of the mufic in the electoral
palace of Hanover about the year 1684. He was the uncle of Carlo Brofchio
Farinelli, the celebrated finger. (See Matthefon, *Vollkomenon Capelmeifter*,
1739.)

A great means of bringing that foreward was the humour of following publick conforts, and it will not be out of the way to deduce them from the beginning. The firft of thofe was in a lane behind Pauls,* where there was a chamber

* This place of entertainment was known by the fign of the Mitre, and was fituated at the north-weft end of St. Paul's Cathedral.   It was eftablifhed early in the reign of Charles the Second by one Robert Hubert, alias Forges, a noted lover of mufic and a colleɐtor of curiofities.   In 1664, he publifhed a fmall pamphlet, entitled, *A Catalogue of the many natural rarities, with great induftry, coft, and thirty years travel into foreign countries, colleɐted by Robert Hubert, alias Forges, Gent. and fworn fervant to his majefty ; and daily to be feen at the place called the Mufick-houfe at the Mitre near the weft end of St. Paul's church.* This colleɐtion was afterwards purchafed by Sir Hans Sloane, and added to his celebrated mufeum.   The "mufick-houfe" was burnt down in the great fire, and afterwards rebuilt.   Sir John Hawkins (*Hift. of Mufic*, vol. iv. p. 379) con- jeɐtures that it was fituated in London-houfe yard, at the north-weft end of St. Paul's churchyard, and on the fpot where formerly ftood the houfe known by the fign of the Goofe and Gridiron, which tradition faid had once been a mufic- houfe.   "It feems," fays Sir John, "that the fucceffor of Hubert was no lover of mufic, but a man of humour, and it is faid that in ridicule of the meetings formerly held there, he chofe for his fign a goofe ftroking the bars of a gridiron with his foot, and called it the Swan and Harp."

Another place of entertainment of the fame kind was the "Mufick-houfe" at Stepney, fituated in the row of houfes fronting the weft end of Stepney church ; it had for a fign the head of Charles II. and was the refort of fea- faring people and others.

Ward (*London Spy*, Part XIV.) has given a particular defcription of a mufic- houfe which he vifited in the courfe of his ramble, furpaffing all of the kind in or about London.   Its fituation was in Wapping, but in what part of that fuburb we are not told.   The fign was that of the Mitre, and by the account this author gives of it, the houfe, which was both a tavern and a mufic-houfe, was a very fpacious and expenfive building.   He fays that the mufic-room was a moft ftately apartment, and that no gilding, carving, painting, or good con-

organ that one Phillips* played upon, and some shopkeepers, and foremen came weekly to sing in consort, and to hear and enjoy ale and tobacco; and after some time the audience grew strong, and one Ben Wallington† got the reputation of a notable base voice, who also set up for a composer, and

trivance were wanting in the decoration of it; the seats, he says, were like the pews in a church, and the upper end being divided by a rail, appeared to him more like a chancel than a music-loft. Of the music he gives but a general account, saying only that it consisted of violins, hautboys, and an organ. The house being a tavern, was accommodated as well to the purpose of drinking, as music; it contained many costly rooms, with whimsical paintings on the wainscotting. The kitchen was railed in to prevent the access to the fire of those who had nothing to do at it, and overhead was what this author calls an harmonious choir of canary birds singing.

Another ancient music-house was that founded in 1683 by Sadler, and still known as Sadler's Wells. Francis Forcer, the composer of various songs in the *Theatre of Music* (printed in the year 1685, 1686, and 1687) was for many years after the death of Sadler, the proprietor of the wells and music-house. He was succeeded by his son who was the first that introduced the diversions of rope-dancing, tumbling, &c.

* John Phillips, a composer of numerous half-sheet songs, at the close of the seventeenth century.

† In Playford's *Catch that Catch can, or the Musical Companion*, 1667, Benjamin Wallington, " Citizen," is mentioned as one of the " endeared friends of the *late* Musick-Society and Meeting in the Old-Jury, London." In the second part of the same work, published in 1672, there is a glee for three voices, of his composition, beginning, " How harmless and free;" and in *New Ayres and Dialogues Composed for Voices and Viols of two, three, and four parts*, published by John Banister and Thomas Low in 1678, there are three duets entitled as follows : " Tis Musick that giveth;" " In a fair pleasant lawn;" " Laurietta once I did." One other specimen, a song " for a bass alone," in *Choice Ayres and Dialogues*, book ii. 1679, comprises all the worthy " citizen's " composition in Print. Roger North has truly characterized them as of " very low excellence."

hath fome fongs in print, but of a very low excelence; and their mufick was cheifly out of Playford's Catch book.*

---

* The popular Catch book of the reign of Charles II. was entitled *Catch that Catch Can, or a Choice Collection of Catches, Rounds, and Canons, for 3 or 4 Voyces. Collected and Publifhed by John Hilton, Batch. in Mufick.* London : printed for *John Benfon* and *John Playford*, and to be fould in St. Dunftan's Churchyard, and in the Inner Temple, neare the Church Doore, 1652. Another edition with confiderable additions was printed in 1658. But it was not until the year after the great fire of 1666 that Playford augmented the collection, and publifhed it under the title of *Catch that Catch Can, or the Mufical Companion. Containing Catches and Rounds for Three and Four Voyces. To which is added a Second Book, containing Dialogues, Glees, Ayres, and Ballads, etc. Some for Two, Three, Four Voyces.* London : printed by *W. Godbid* for *J. Playford*, at his Shop in the Inner Temple, 1667. Playford dedicates this volume " To his endeared Friends of the late Mufic-Society and Meeting in the Old-Jury, London," one of the earlieft mufic meetings or focieties of which we have any record. Thefe friends were, Charles Pigon, Efq., Mr. John Tempeft, Gent., Mr. Herbert Pelham, Gent., Mr. John Pelling, Citizen, Mr. Benjamin Walington, Citizen, Mr. George Piggot, Gent., Mr. Francis Piggot, Citizen, and Mr. John Rogers, Gent. In this work there are no fewer than 143 catches, 3 dialogues for 2 voices, 11 glees for 2 and 3 voices, 53 ayres, ballads, and fongs for 3 and 4 voices, and 8 Italian and Latin fongs, in all 218 compofitions. It is confidered the earlieft work in which the glee is mentioned ; but this is an error, as that term is ufed for fome two-part fongs in *Select Ayres and Dialogues*, publifhed by Playford in 1659. In 1673 Playford produced a new edition of the *Mufical Companion*, to which he added 51 glees and fongs. It was ufhered into the world by commendatory verfes written by Matthew Locke, C. Pidgeon, and Thomas Jordan, the city poet. In 1685, the *Second Part of the Mufical Companion* appeared, containing " Seventy New Catches and Songs," many of them printed from the author's own copies." This was reprinted in 1687, with " fome old revifed fongs fometime fung at the Theatres." Among the latter is the ftill celebrated fong, " Mad Tom," erroneoufly attributed to Purcell, but compofed by Giovanni Coperario for a mafk performed at Gray's Inn in 1600. Between 1685 (the date of the firft edition) and 1730 this work paffed through *ten* editions. The title page to the fourth edition (which was

But this ſhewed an inclination of the citizens to follow muſick. And the ſame was confirmed by many litle entertainments, the maſters voluntarily made for their ſcollars, for
being knowne they were alwais crowded.

The next eſſay was of the elder Baniſter, who had a good
theatricall vein, and in compoſition had a lively ſtyle peculiar
to himſelf. He procured a large room in Whitefryars, neer
the Temple back gate, and made a large raiſed box for the
muſitians, whoſe modeſty required curtaines.* The room

much enlarged from the former) ſtates it to have been " Publiſhed chiefly for
the encouragement of the Muſical Societies which will be ſpeedily ſet up in all
the chief Cities and Towns in England." It is dated 1701. This edition contains 53 catches by Henry Purcell, and 11 by Dr. Blow.

* John Baniſter, the originator of theſe concerts, ſucceeded the celebrated
Baltzar as leader of the King's band of violins in 1663. He is reported to have
been ſent by Charles II. to France for improvement, but ſoon after his return,
was diſmiſſed the King's ſervice for ſaying that the Engliſh violins were better
than the French. Pepys, in his intereſting Diary, under the date Feb. 20,
1666-7, ſays, " They talk how the King's violin Banniſter, is mad; that the
King hath a Frenchman come to be chief of ſome part of the King's muſique."
The Frenchman appointed by Charles was the impudent pretender Louis
Grabu, of whom Pepys has left us the following notice (*Diary*, Oct. 1. 1667) :
" To White Hall, and there in the Boarded Gallery did hear the Muſick with
which the King is preſented this night by Monſieur Grebus, the Maſter of his
Muſick : both inſtrumental (I think twenty-four violins) and vocall; and an
Engliſh Song upon Peace. But, God forgive me ! I never was ſo little pleaſed
with a concert of muſick in my life. The manner of ſetting of words, and re-
peating them out of order, and that with a number of voices, makes me ſick,
the whole deſign of vocall muſick being loſt by it. Here was a great preſs of
people ; but I did not ſee many pleaſed with it, only the inſtrumental muſick he
had brought by practice to play very juſt."

Baniſter commenced his concerts in 1672, and the lovers of muſic were

was rounded with seats and small tables, alehous fashion. One shilling was the price, and call for what you pleased; there was very good musick, for Banister found means to procure the best hands in towne, and some voices to come and

invited by advertisements in the *London Gazette*, the forms of which were as follows :—

" These are to give notice, that at Mr. John Banister's house (now called the Musick-school) over against the George tavern in White Fryers, this present Monday, will be musick performed by excellent masters, beginning precisely at 4 of the clock in the afternoon, and every afternoon for the future, precisely at the same hour" (*London Gazette*, No. 742. *Dec.* 30, 1672).

" At the Musick-school in White-Fryers, this present Monday, several new Ayres will be performed, beginning at seven of the clock in the evening; the usual publick room to be wholly abated, and the other rooms and boxes the one halfe; this is to continue till Michaelmas next" (*London Gazette*, No. 878. *January* 10, 1674).

" On Thursday next, the 14th instant, at the Academy in Little Lincoln's-Inn Fields, will begin the first part of the Parley of Instruments, composed by Mr. John Banister, and perform'd by eminent masters, at six o'clock, and to continue nightly, as shall by bill or otherwise be notifi'd. The tickets are to be deliver'd out from one of the clock till five every day, and not after." (*Lond. Gaz.* No. 1154. *Dec.* 11, 1676.)

" On Thursday next, the 22d of this instant November, at the Musick-school in Essex Buildings, over-against St. Clement's church in the strand, will be continued a consort of vocal and instrumental musick, beginning at five of the clock every evening, composed by Mr. John Banister" (*Lond. Gaz.* No. 1356. *Nov.* 18, 1678).

Many similar advertisements may be seen in the *London Gazette* from 1672 to 1678, from which it appears that Banister continued these concerts from their commencement till near the period of his decease, which occurred in 1679. He was buried in the Cloisters of Westminster Abbey. In 1678 (the year of the close of Banister's concerts) the club or private concert established by John Britton, the musical small-coal man, in Clerkenwell, had its beginning and continued till 1714.

performe there, and there wanted no variety of humour, for Banifter himfelf (*inter alia*) did wonders upon a flageolett to a thro' Bafe, and the feverall mafters had their folos. This continued full one winter, and more I remember not.

54.
The Gen-
tlemens
Meeting.

There was a fociety of gentlemen of good efteem, whom I fhall not name, for fome of them as I hear are ftill living, that ufed to meet often for confort after Baptift's manner, and falling into a weekly courfe, and performing exceeding well, with Bafs violins (a cours inftrument as it was then, which they ufed to hire) their friends and acquaintance, were admitted, and by degrees, as the fame of their meeting fpread, fo many auditors came that their room was crowded; and to prevent that inconvenience, they took a room in a taverne in Fleet ftreet, and the taverner pretended to make formall feats, and to take money, and then the fociety difbanded. But the taverner finding the fweets of vinting wine and taking money, hired mafters to play, and made a pecuniary confort of it, to which for the reputation of the mufick, numbers of people of good fafhion and quallity repaired.

55.
The York
Mufick
houfe, and
how failed.

The mafters of mufick finding that money was to be got this way, determined to take the bufinefs into their owne hands; and it proceeded fo far, that in York buildings,* a

---

* About the year 1680, the principal profefïors of mufic in London had a room built and fitted up for concerts in Villiers ftreet, York buildings, "where the beft compofitions and performers of the time were heard by the firft people in London." This was called the *Mufic Meeting*. The room was fituated on the right hand fide of the ftreet, near the bottom, and adjoining what is ftill

fabrick was reared and furnifhed on purpofe for publick mufick. And there was nothing of mufick valued in towne, but

---

called the " water-office." It was ufed for concerts down to the middle of the
laft century, when the attractions of other rifing " mufick-rooms " caufed it to
be entirely abandoned, and about the year 1768 it was pulled down and two
fmall houfes erected upon its fite. The following are a few of the moft inter-
efting advertifements which appeared in the daily papers fhortly after the eftablifhment of the " mufick-meeting."

" The Confort of vocal and inftrumental mufick, lately held in York Buildings, will be performed again at the fame place and hour as formerly, on Monday next, being Eafter Monday, by the command and for the entertainment of
her Royal Highnefs the Princefs of Denmark" (*London Gazette*, No. 2651.
April 9, 1691).

" The Italian lady (that is lately come over, that is fo famous for her finging)
has been reported that fhe will fing no more in the confort in York-buildings :
This is to give notice, that next Tuefday, being the 10th inftant, fhe will fing
in the Confort in York Buildings, and fo continue during this feafon" (*Lond.
Gaz.* No. 2834. *Jan.* 9, 1692).

" Thefe are to give notice that the mufick meeting in which the Italian
woman fings, will be held every Tuefday in York buildings, and Thurfdays in
Freeman's yard in Cornhill, near the Royall Exchange" (*Lond. Gaz.* No. 2838.
Jan. 23, 1692).

" At the confort-room in York-buildings, on this prefent Thurfday, at the
ufual hour will be performed Mr. Purcell's Song compofed for St. Cecilia's Day
in the year 1692, together with fome other compofitions of his, both vocal and
inftrumental, for the entertainment of his Highnefs Prince Lewis of Baden"
(*Lond. Gaz.* No. 2943. *Jan.* 25, 1693).

" Seignor Tofi's confort of mufick will begin on Monday the 30th inft. in
York-buildings, at 8 o'clock in the evening, to continue weekly all the winter"
(*Lond. Gaz.* No. 2917. *Oct.* 25, 1693).

In November 1702 a concert at York Buildings is advertifed in the Daily
Courant " by performers lately come from Rome." The advertifement is
feveral times repeated in this and the following month. The next year, 1703,
Sig. Gafparini and Sig. Petto performed together at the " confort in York-buildings," and Sig. Saggione " lately arrived from Italy" compofes. In March of

was to be heard there. It was called the Mufick-Meeting; and all the quallity and *beau mond* repaired to it, but the plan of this project was not fo well layd as ought to have bin, for the time of their beginning was inconfiftent with the park and the playhoufes, which had a ftronger attraction. And what was wors, the mafters undertakers were a rope of fand, not under the rule or order of any perfon, and every one foreward to advance his owne talents, and fpightfull to each other, and out of emulation fubftracting their fkill in performing; all which together fcandalized the company, and poyfoned the entertainment. Befides the whole was without defigne or order; for one mafter brings a confort with fuges,

---

the fame year Sig. Francefco advertifes a concert " with Songs by Signora Anna lately arrived from Rome." At the beginning of the eighteenth century foreign compofers and fingers of all kinds flocked into England in abundance, and the concerts in York buildings feem generally to have been chofen as their firft effay for public favour.

In 1710, Sir Richard Steele became proprietor of the concert-room in York-buildings, when three obfcure muficians, Clayton, Haym, and Dieupart (who had loft their influence at the Opera houfe, through the arrival of Handel) folicited fubfcriptions and endeavoured to eftablifh a feries of concerts upon the plan of the former " mufick-meetings." But the glory of York-buildings had departed, and it does not appear (although they were abetted and patronized by Sir Richard Steele, fee *Spectator*, No. 158 and 178) that their plans took effect.

In April 1732, the " Daily Journal" announces: " Never performed in public, at the great room in Villar's-ftreet, York-buildings, by the beft vocal and inftrumental mufick, Efther, an Oratorio, or facred drama, will be performed, on Thurfday, April 20th as it was compofed for the Moft Noble James, Duke of Chandos, by George Frederick Handel. Each ticket five fhillings." This appears to be the laft event worth recording in the hiftory of this once famous mufic-room.

another ſhews his guifts in a ſolo upon the violin, another ſings, and then a famous lutiniſt comes foreward, and in this manner changes followed each other, with a full ceſſation of the muſick between every one, and a gabble and buſtle while they changed places; whereas all entertainments of this kind ought to be projected as a drama, ſo as all the members ſhall uninteruptedly follow in order, and having a true connexion, ſet off each other. It is no wonder that the playhouſes got ground, and as they ordered the matter, ſoon routed this Muſick-meeting.

It had bin ſtrange if the gentlemen of the theaters had ſate ſtill all this while, ſeeing as they ſay a pudding creep, that is a violent inclination in the towne to follow muſick, and they not ſerve themſelves of it. Therefore Mr. Betterton, who was the chief ingineer of the ſtage, contrived a ſort of plays, which were called Operas, but had been more properly ſtyled Semi-operas, for they conſiſted of half muſick, and half drama. The cheif of theſe were Circe,* The Fayery

56. The Semi-Operas at the Theatres.

---

* The tragedy of *Circe* was written by Dr. Charles Davenant (eldeſt ſon of Sir William Davenant) and produced at the Duke of York's theatre in 1676. Downes (*Roſcius Anglicanus*) calls it an " Opera," and ſays, " All the Muſick was ſet by Mr. Baniſter, and being well performed, it anſwered the expectation of the Company." A portion of the muſic, conſiſting of the firſt act only, is preſerved in a MS. volume now in the library of the Sacred Harmonic Society. One of the Songs is printed in the ſecond book of *Choice Ayres and Songs,* 1679. From a peruſal of theſe ſpecimens, the editor is inclined to give Baniſter a much higher ſtation among the dramatic compoſers of this country than has hitherto been aſſigned him.

Queen,* Dioclefian,† and King Arthur ;‡ which latter was compofed by Purcell, and is unhappyly loft. Thefe were

---

* The operatic play of *The Fairy Queen* was an anonymous adaptation of Shakefpeare's *Midfummer Night's Dream* produced at the theatre in the Haymarket in 1692. "This in ornaments," fays Downes, (*Rofcius Anglicanus*) "was fuperior to the other two (i. e. *King Arthur and Dioclefian*); efpecially in cloaths for all the Singers and Dancers ; Scenes, Machines, and decorations ; all moft profufely fet off, and excellently perform'd : chiefly the inftrumentall and vocal part compof'd by the faid Mr. Purcell, and dances by Mr. Prieft. The Court and Town were wonderfully fatisfy'd with it ; but the expences in fetting it out being fo great, the Company got very little by it." The mufic to this play is lefs known than any other of Purcell's dramatic works. A collection of " the favorite fongs" appeared in the year of its performance, and fome few others may be found fcattered through the various collections of the time, but as a whole it is to this day *unknown*. This may be accounted for by the following advertifement, which appeared in the *London Gazette* of Oct. 13, 1700 : " The Score of Mufick for the Fairy Queen, fet by the late Mr. Henry Purcell, and belonging to the Patentees of the Theatre Royal in Covent Garden, London, being loft by his death ; Whofoever brings the faid Score, or a copy thereof to Mr. Zachary Baggs, Treafurer of the faid Theatre, fhall have 20 Guineas Reward." This advertifement was repeated in the fame paper of the 20th, but we have no means of afcertaining whether it was recovered. The probability is, as the opera was not revived, that it was not.

† *Dioclefian, or the Prophetefs,* was an adaptation from Beaumont and Fletcher's play of the *Prophetefs,* by Betterton. It was produced at the Queen's theatre in 1690, and the " vocal and inftrumental mufic," was, as Downes expreffes it, " done by Mr. Purcell." He alfo tells us (*Rofcius Anglicanus*) that " it gratify'd the expectation of Court and City ; and got the author great reputation." In the following year, 1691, Purcell printed the mufic in fcore with a Dedication to Charles, Duke of Somerfet. This opera was afterwards " newly revived" when Purcell made confiderable alterations and additions.

‡ Dryden's opera of *King Arthur* was produced at the Queen's theatre in 1691, with the unrivalled mufic of Henry Purcell, and both Downes and Cibber record its " great fuccefs." The honourable writer could fcarcely be unaware that the *Fairy Queen* and *Dioclefian* were alfo the compofition of Pur-

followed at firſt, but by an error of mixing two capitall enter-
teinments, could not ſtand long. For ſome that would come
to the play hated the muſick, and others that were very de-
ſirous of the muſick, would not bear the interruption that ſo
much rehearſall gave; ſo that it is beſt to have either by it
ſelf intire.

But nothing advanced muſick more in this age then the
patronage of the nobility, and men of fortunes, for they became encouragers of it by great liberallitys, and countenance
to the profeſſors. And this was made very publick by a con-
tribution amongſt them, to be given as a premio to him that
ſhould beſt entertein them in a ſolemne conſort; and divers
of the maſters enterd the liſts, and their performances were
in the theater ſucceſſively heard, and the victorys decided by
the judgment of the ſubſcribers.* But this method gave no

57.
Of the Prize
Muſick, and
the ill effects
of competi-
tion.

cell ! But his teſtimony, regarding King Arthur, points to the concluſion, which
is too well confirmed by other evidence, that the complete ſcore of that opera
ſpeedily vaniſhed. (See the edition of *King Arthur* printed for the members
of the *Muſical Antiquarian Society*.) The ſcore of King Arthur was probably
loſt from the theatre at the ſame time with that of the *Fairy Queen*. Five
pieces are ſtill unknown at the preſent day.

* In the *London Gazette*, No. 3585, for March 21, 1699, appeared the
following advertiſement: " Several perſons of quality having, for the encouragement of muſick advanced 200 guineas, to be diſtributed in 4 prizes, the
firſt of 100, the ſecond of 50, the third of 30, and the fourth of 20 guineas, to
ſuch maſters as ſhall be adjudged to compoſe the beſt ; this is therefore to give
notice, that thoſe who intend to put in for the prizes, are to repair to Jacob
Tonſon, at Gray's-Inn-gate, before Eaſter-day next, where they may be further
informed." It is conjectured, from the dedication of the *Orpheus Britanicus*,
book ii. that the Earl of Halifax was a liberal contributor to the fund out of

fatisfaction; for the Lords & the reft that fubfcribed (as the good King Charles the Second) had ears, but not artificiall ones, and thofe were neceffary to warrant the authority of fuch a court of juftice. I will not fuppofe, as fome did, that making intereft as for favour and partiallity influenced thefe determinations; but it is certain, that the comunity of the mafters were not of the fame opinion with them. And fo inftead of incouraging the endeavours of all, the happy victor onely was pleafed, and all the reft were difcontented, and fome who thought they deferved better, were almoft ready to relinquifh the faculty; and Mr. G. Finger,* a ger-

---

which thefe fums were propofed to be paid (fee Hawkins, *Hift of Muf.* iv. 540). The poem chofen as the fubject of the mufical compofition was the *Judgment of Paris*, written by Congreve. Weldon, Eccles, Daniel Purcell, and Godfrey Finger were the fuccefsful competitors. Weldon obtaining the firft prize, Eccles the fecond, Daniel Purcell the third, and Finger, the beft mufician perhaps among the candidates, the fourth. Jeremiah Clark, being afked why he did not compofe for the prize, made anfwer, that "the nobility were to be the judges," leaving the querift to draw his own inference. Thefe compofitions were performed on the ftage at Drury Lane and Dorfet Gardens, in the years 1701-4. Finger's Ode appears to have been fo ill received that the compofer left this country in difguft foon after its performance. In the Harleian MS. No. 5961. (art. 241) is preferved the printed ticket "For the Mufick prize Compof'd by Mr. Finger. Friday, March the 28, 1701." Eccles' and Purcell's mufic to the *Judgment of Paris* was printed in fcore by Walfh; the other two compofitions exift only in manufcript. Weldon's glee "Let Ambition fire thy mind" is the only portion of his prize ode now known. The original MS. occurred in the Rev. J. Parker's fale, 1813 (lot 37), and in Shade's catalogue of old mufic for the following year.

    * Godfrey Finger was a voluminous compofer of vocal and inftrumental mufic, for many years refident in England. He was a native of Olmutz, in Moravia, not of Silefia, as generally ftated. In 1685, he received the appoint-

man, and a good mufitian, one of the competitors, who had
refided in England many years, went away upon it, declaring

---

ment of Chapel Mafter to King James II. and in 1688 he printed *Sonatæ XII.
pro diverfis Inftrumentis quarum tres priores pro Violino et Viola di Gamba, prox-
imæ tres pro ii Violinis et Viola di Baſſo, tres fequentis pro iii Violinis, reliquæ
pro ii Violinis et Viola, omnes ad Baſi Continuam pro Organo ſeu Clavycymbalo
formantur. Authore Godefrido Finger, Olmutio-Moravo, Capellæ Sereniſſimi
Regis Magnæ Britaniæ Muſico. Opus primum.* Anno 1688. This rare work
is embelliſhed with a portrait of the author in the act of kneeling before a
buſt of his Majeſty, to whom the Sonatas are dedicated. In 1690 he printed
*VI. Sonatas or Solo's ; three for a Violin, and three for a Flute, with a Thorough
Baſs for the Harpſychord: Moſt humbly Dedicated to the Right Honourable
Charles Earl of Mancheſter, Viſcount Mandevil Baron Kimbolton and Lord
Lieutenant of the County of Huntingdon, by the author Godfry Finger.* No
printer or publiſher's name is attached to this work, from which we may conjecture it to have been a private publication. In the following year he publiſhed,
in conjunction with John Baniſter (a fon of the celebrated violin player before
mentioned), *Ayres, Chacones, Diviſions, and Sonatas, for Violins and Flutes.*
They are advertiſed in the " London Gazette" of November 5, 1691, to be
ſold at " Mr. Baniſter's houfe, in Brownlow-ſtreet, Drury-lane." Shortly after
this date he joined Godfrey Keller in publiſhing *A Set of Sonatas in Five parts
for Flutes and Hautboys* (fee Henry Playford's *General Catalogue,* 1701). The
titles of various other inſtrumental works of this author are briefly given in the
Amſterdam catalogues. In 1693 he compoſed the Ode for St. Cecilia's Day,
which was thus advertiſed for performance in the " London Gazette" of Feb. 1,
for that year: " At the Confort in York-buildings on Monday next the 5th
inſtant, will be performed Mr. Finger's St. Cecilia's Song, intermixed with a
variety of new muſick, at the ordinary rates."

Finger is chiefly regarded as a compoſer of inſtrumental muſic, and the fact
of his having been a large contributor to the dramatic muſic of his day has been
entirely overlooked by muſical antiquaries and hiſtorians. The plays for which
he compoſed the muſic (as far as the Editor has yet diſcovered) are as follows :
The Wives Excuſe, written by Southerne, and performed at Drury Lane, 1692.
Love for Love, written by Congreve, performed at Lincoln's Inn Fields, 1695.
The Loves of Mars and Venus, written by Motteaux, performed at Lincoln's

that he thought he was to compofe mufick for men, and not for boys. So much a miftake it is to force artifts upon a competition, for all but one are fure to be malecontents. And more happened upon a competition for an Organ at the Temple Church, for which the two competitors, the beft artifts in Europe, Smith and Harris, were but juft not ruined.*

Inn Fields, 1696. *The Anatomift, or Sham Doctor*, written by Ravenfcroft, performed at Lincoln's Inn Fields, 1697. *The Humours of the Age*, written by T. Baker, performed at Drury Lane, 1701. *Love at a lofs*, written by Mrs. Trotter, performed at Drury Lane, 1701. *Love makes a Man, or the Fops fortune*, written by Cibber, performed at Drury Lane, 1701. *Sir Harry Wildhair*, written by Farquhar, performed at Drury Lane, 1701.

Several of Finger's fongs may be found in Playford and Carr's various collections. In the *Thefaurus Muficus* (book iv. p. 5) is "A Song upon Mrs. Bracegirdle's acting Marcella in Don Quixote;" and in the fame book (p. 10) is "A new Song fung by the Boy at the Confort in Duke-ftreet, Covent Garden," both fet to mufic by Finger. After the ill fuccefs of his Ode (fee previous note) Finger returned to Germany, and according to Matthefon (*Grundlage einer Ehrenpforte, Hamb.* 1740) in 1702, received the appointment of Chamber-mufician to Sophia Charlotte, Queen of Pruffia. In 1717 (fee the fame writer), he was appointed Chapel-mafter to the Court of Gotha.

* This celebrated contention between Smith and Harris was carried on with fuch fpirit, not to fay violence, as perhaps never happened before or fince on a fimilar occafion. The circumftances connected with the cafe are briefly thefe. About the latter end of King Charles the Second's reign (i. e. 1681) the Societies of the Temple determined to have an organ as complete as poffible erected in their church. They received propofals from Smith and Harris. Thefe diftinguifhed artifts were fupported by the recommendation of fuch an equal number of powerful friends and celebrated organifts, that they were unable to determine among themfelves which to employ. They therefore told the candidates, if each of them would erect an organ in different parts of the church, they would retain that which, in the greateft number of excellencies, fhould be

But as yet wee have given no account of the decadence of the French muſick, and the Itallian coming in its room.

58.
Italian Mu-
ſick, and the
Caraƈtar of
the elder N.
Matteis.

allowed to deſerve the preference. Smith and Harris agreed to this propoſal, and in about nine months each had, with the utmoſt exertion of his abilities, an inſtrument ready for trial. Dr. Tudway, their contemporary, and the intimate acquaintance of both, ſays that Dr. Blow and Purcell, then in their prime, per-formed on Father Smith's organ on appointed days, and diſplayed its excellen-cies; and, till the other was heard, every one believed that this muſt be choſen. Harris employed Baptiſte Draghi, organiſt to Queen Catherine, (not the cele-brated Jean Baptiſte Lulli, as generally ſtated,) " to touch his organ," which brought it into favour; and thus " they continued vying with each other for near a twelvemonth." At length Harris challenged Father Smith, to make certain additional reed ſtops, within a given time: theſe were the *vox humana*, *cromorne*, (not *cremona*, as Dr. Tudway calls it,) the *double courtel*, or double baſſoon, and ſome others. Theſe ſtops, which were newly invented, or at leaſt new to Engliſh ears, gave great delight to the crowds who attended the trials; and the imitations were ſo exaƈt and pleaſing on both ſides, that it was difficult to determine who had beſt ſucceeded. At length the deciſion was left to Lord Chief Juſtice Jefferies, afterwards King James the Second's pliant Chancellor, who was of the Inner Temple; and he terminated the controverſy in favour of Father Smith. Old Roſeingrave aſſured Dr. Burney that the partizans for each candidate, in the fury of their zeal, proceeded to the moſt miſchievous and un-warrantable aƈts of hoſtilities; and that in the night preceding the laſt trial of the reed ſtops, the friends of Harris cut the bellows of Smith's organ in ſuch a manner, that when the time came for playing upon it, no wind could be con-veyed into the wind-cheſt. Harris's organ, after its rejeƈtion at the Temple, was part of it ereƈted at St. Andrew's, Holborn, and part in the Cathedral of Chriſt-Church, Dublin. The latter was removed by Byfield about 1750, and ultimately placed in one of the churches at Wolverhampton. Smith ſeems to have excelled in the diapaſon or foundation ſtops; Harris principally in the reed ſtops. The latter appears to have been ſenſible of the ſuperiority of Smith's diapaſons, for at the laſt trial of the Temple organ, he challenged him to make, not diapaſon, but reed ſtops, which Smith accepted, and as we have ſeen, car-ried the palm againſt him. The ſwell was added to the Temple organ by

This happened by degrees, and the overture was by accident, for the coming over of Sig. Nicolai Matteis gave the firſt ſtart.* He was an excellent muſitian, and performed wonderfully upon the violin. His manner was ſingular, but in one reſpeĉt excelled all that had bin knowne before in England, which was the arcata. His ſtaccatas, tremolos, deviſions, and indeed his whole manner was ſurpriſing, and every ſtroke of his was a mouthfull. Beſides, all that he played was of his owne compoſition, which ſhowed him a very exquiſite

Byfield about 1750. This important improvement upon the old organs was invented by Jordan in 1715 (ſee his Advertiſement in the original edition of the Speĉtator). For particulars of the recent alterations in this organ ſee Mr. Burge's *Account of the Reſtoration and Repairs of the Temple Church*, 1843, pp. 68—73. Smith's principal organs are thoſe at St. Paul's (ereĉted 1697); Durham Cathedral; Chriſt Church, and St. Mary's, Oxford; Trinity College, Cambridge; Southwell Minſter; St. Mary's, Woolnoth; St. Mary at Hill; St. Martin's, Ludgate hill; St. Clement Danes; and Trinity Church, Hull. The latter is ſaid to have been originally intended for St. Paul's Cathedral in addition to the preſent inſtrument. Harris's principal organs are thoſe at St. Dionis, Backchurch; St. Lawrence, near Guildhall; St. Sepulchre's; St. Giles's, Cripplegate; St. Andrew's, Underſhaft; St. Bride's; Chriſt Church, Newgate Street; St. James's, Piccadilly, &c. &c.

* Nicola Matteis came to England about the year 1672, and the earlieſt account we have of his wonderful powers on the violin is given us by the goſſiping Pepys: "Novemb. 19, 1674. I heard that ſtupendous violin, Sig. Nicholao (with other rare muſicians), whom I never heard mortal man exceed on that inſtrument. He had a ſtroak ſo ſweete, and made it ſpeak like the voice of a man, and, when he pleaf'd, like a conſort of ſeverall inſtruments. He did wonders upon a note, and was an excellent compoſer. Here was alſo that rare luteniſt Dr. Walgrave; but nothing approached the violin in Nicholao's hand. He plaied ſuch raviſhing things as aſtoniſh'd us all." Matteis is ſuppoſed to have been the inventor of the half ſhift on the violin. It is alſo claimed by Geminiani and Vivaldi (ſee Burney, *Hiſt of Muſic*, iii. 561 *note*).

harmonift, and of a boundlefs fancy, and invention. And by all that I have knowne of him and other mufick of Itally, I cannot but judge him to have bin fecond to Corelli. When he came over firft he was very poor, but not fo poor as proud, which was the reafon that kept him back, fo that he had no acquaintance for a long time, but a merchant or two who patronized him. And he valuing himfelf at an exceffive rate, fquezed confiderable fums out of them. By degrees he became more taken notice of; he was heard play at Court, but his manner did not take, and he behaved himfelf faftoufly; no perfon muft whifper while he played, which fort of attention had not bin the fafhion at Court. It was faid that a nobleman, the Duke of Richmond (I think it was), would have given him a penfion, but he did not like his way of playing, and would needs have a Page of his fhew him the beft manner, and he for the jeft fake, condefcended to learne of the Page, but learnt fo faft that he foon outrun his mafter in his owne way. In fhort, he was fo outrageous in his demands, efpecially for his high peices folos, that very few would come up to him, and he continued low and obfcure a long time.

And he had continued fo but for two or three vertuofos, who were Dr. Walgrave,* a prodigy of an arch-lutanift, Sir Roger Leftrange,† an expert violift, and Mr. Bridgman, the

59.
Sufteined and civilized by Dr. Walgrave.

---

* A celebrated dilletanti mentioned in the previous extract from Pepys' Diary.

† Sir Roger L'Eftrange was born in the year 1616. He was the author of

under-fecretary, a thro-bafe man upon the harpficord. Thefe got him into their acquaintance, and courting him in his owne way by difcours, fhewing him the temper of the Englifh, who if they were humoured, would be liberall, but if not humoured would doe nothing at all; And by putting on an air of complaifance, and doing as they defired, he would not want imployment or mony. They brought him by degrees into fuch good temper as made him efteemed and fought after, and having got many fcollars, tho at moderate rates, his purs filled apace, which confirmed his converfion, and he continued very tractable as long as he lived. And he found

---

numerous pamphlets and periodical publications, and Licenfer of the Prefs to Charles II. and his fucceffor. He was alfo M.P. for Winchefter in James II.'s Parliament. His performance on the violin at the houfe of Hingfton, in St. James's Park, before the Protector Oliver Cromwell gained him, from his political antagonifts, the nickname of "Oliver's Fidler." In a pamphlet, entitled "Truth and Loyalty vindicated," 1662, he clears himfelf from the imputation which this reproachful appellation was intended to fix upon him, in the following words: "Concerning the ftory of the fiddle, this I fuppofe might be the rife of it. Being in St. James's Park, I heard an organ touched in a little low room of one Mr. Hinckfon's; I went in, and found a private company of five or fix perfons: they defired me to take up a viole and bear a part; I did fo, and that a part too, not much to advance the reputation of my cunning. By and by, without the leaft colour of a defign or expectation, in comes Cromwell. He found us playing, and as I remember fo he left us." There is a pamphlet in the Britifh Mufeum, printed in 1683, attacking him under the title of "The Loyal Obfervator; or Hiftorical Memoirs of the Life and Actions of Roger the Fidler; alias the Obfervator." Ned Ward, in his account of Britton the fmall-coal man's concerts, (*Satirical Reflections on Clubs*, 1709,) fays, "this club was firft begun, or at leaft confirmed, by Sir Roger L'Eftrange, a very mufical gentleman, and who had a tolerable perfection on the bafs-viol." He died in 1704, and was buried in the Church of St. Giles's in the Fields.

out a way of getting mony which was perfectly new. For feeing his leffons (which were all duos) take with his fcollars, and that moft gentlemen defired them, he was at fome charge to have them graven in copper, and printed in oblong octavos, and this was the beginning of ingraving mufick in England.* And of thefe leffons he made books, and prefented them, well bound, to moft of the lovers, which brought him the 3, 4, and 5 ginnys. And the incouragement was fo great, that he made four of them.† And a cappriccio came in his crowne

---

* Roger North is not quite correct in this ftatement. The firft mufic book engraved on copper plate in England was publifhed in 1611, under the follow-ing title: *Parthenia, or the Maydenhead of the firft muficke that ever was printed for the Virginals, Compofed by three famous Mafters, William Byrd, Dr. John Bull, and Orlando Gibbons, Gentlemen of his Majefties Moft Illuftrious Chappell. Ingraven by William Hole. Lond. print. for Mris. Dor. Evans. Cum privilegio. Are to be fould by G. Lowe, prinr. in Loathberry.* This rare work is dedicated " To the High and Mighty and Magnificent Princes, Frederick Elector Palatine of the Reine; and his betrothed Lady Elizabeth, the only daughter of my Lord the King." Profeffor Taylor (*Three Inagural Lectures*, p. 32) has quoted the dedication at length, but has erroneoufly applied it to Queen Elizabeth before fhe afcended the throne, and during the time that a treaty of marriage was con-templated between her and the Elector Palatine. There were many later edi-tions (from the fame plates) down to the year 1659, but that of 1611 was un-doubtedly the firft. This work was followed by another, engraved in a fimilar manner, entitled, *Parthenia In-Violata; or Mayden-Muficke for the Virginalls and Bafs-Viol. Selected out of the Compofitions of the moft famous in that Arte By Robert Hole, and Confecrated to all true Lovers and Practicers therof. Printed at London for John Pyper, and are to be fold at his fhopp at Pauls gate next unto cheapfide at the croffe Keies.* John Playford publifhed his *Muficks Hand-Maid* from copper-plates in 1663; and Matthew Locke his *Melothefia* in 1673. The old practice of printing from types however continued in general ufe till the commencement of the following century.

† The two firft of thefe books confift of *Preludes, Allemands, Sarabands, Cou-*

to make the like for Paris, as he did, and went over to fiddle it there, but foon came back *infecta*. For tho he pretended to compofe in the ftyle of all nations, and of the French in particular, he foon found that piftolls did not walk fo faft as ginnys. But he vended his copys (for they were not printed) in Ingland to very good purpofe. He made another book, which was defigned to teach compofition, ayre, and to play from a thro-bafs.* And his examplars were for the Guittarre, of which inftrument he was a confumate mafter, and had the force upon it to ftand in Confort againft an Harpficord. This book was printed, but few of the copys are to be found. Thefe books of his were of grounds and fhort peices or leffons onely; his full conforts and folos were not printed, and I think are very fcarce, if at all to be met with. But one thing to be obferved was very extraordinary, which is

---

rants, *Gigues, Divifions on Grounds,* and *double compofitions fitted to all hands and capacities.* The third book has for title, *Ayres for the Violin, to wit :* Preludes, *Fugues, Allemands, Sarabands, Courants, Gigues, Fancies, Divifions, and likewife other Paffages, Introductions, and Fuges, for fingle and double Stops ; with Divifions fomewhat more artificial for the Improvement of the Hand upon the Bafeviol or Harpfichord.* The fourth book is entitled, *Other Ayres and Pieces, for the Violin, Bafe-viol, and Harpfichord, fomewhat more difficult and artificial than the former ; compofed for the Practice and Service of greater Mafters upon thofe Inftruments.* Thefe books are all printed in fmall oblong form without date or printer's name. Imperfect copies are preferved in the Mufic-School, Oxford.

* The following is the title of this rare volume : *The Falfe Confonances of Mufick, Or Inftructions for the playing a true Bafe upon the Guittarre, with Choice Examples and cleare Directions to enable any man in a fhort time to play all Muficall Ayres. A great help likewife to thofe that would play exactly upon the Harpficord, Lute, or Bafe-Violl, fhewing the delicacy of all Accords, and how to apply them in their proper places ; In four Parts, by Nicola Matteis.*

that while folks were acquainted with his manner of playing, as he often did in full company's, out of his books, no perfon pretended to doe the like, for none could command that fullnefs, grace, and truth, as he did, fo that in his time his books fuffered for the difficulty, and fince as much becaus unknowne, and yet there is nothing in them puzling or feeming difficult for the hand, and now no perfon can have an idea of this that I have obferved here, who was not a wittnefs of his playing in perfon. In fhort his books, well obferved, are a fufficient tutor of artfull compofition.*

Another obfervation of him was that when an affembly for mufick was, as divers were, appointed, and he onely to entertein the company, having his minifters, Waldegrave, Leftrange, and Bridgman about him, and flaming as I have feen him, in a good humour, he hath held the company by the ears with that force and variety for more then an hour toge-

60.
Well attended to.

* " Though the compofitions of the elder Matteis," fays Burney, " would not now appear very original or elaborate, yet they ftill retain fuch a degree of facility and elegance, and fo many traits of the beautiful melody that was floating about Italy during the youth of Corelli, as render them far from contemptible." (*Hift. of Mufic*, iii. 516.)

The vocal mufic of Matteis is not known at the prefent day. He compofed an Ode for the Feftival of St. Cecilia in 1695, but it was never printed. The following advertifements are from the popular newfpaper of the day:—

" The mufick that was performed on St. Cecilia's Day, compofed by Signior Nicola, will be performed on Thurfday night, in York-buildings, being the 7th inftant" (*Lond. Gaz.* No. 3250. *Jan.* 4, 1696).

" This prefent Monday, being the 30th of May, Mr. Nichola's confort of vocal and inftrumental will be performed in York-buildings" (*Lond. Gaz.* No. 3396. *May* 30, 1698).

ther, that there was fcarce a whifper in the room, tho filled with company. In fhort, waiving the mention of other excellencies in particular, he fell into fuch credit and imployment, that he took a great hous, and after the mode of his country lived luxurioufly, which brought difeafes upon him of which he dyed. He left a fon Nicholas, whom he taught upon the violin from his cradle; and I have feen the boy in coats play to his fathers Guittarre. He grew up, and was a celebrated mafter upon the violin in London for divers years; he being invited went over into Germany, and hath ever fince bin there, and now refides at Vienna, in full payment for all the mafters wee have received out of thofe countrys.*

61.
Italian Mufick, and Corelli.

After this wee cannot wonder, that among the courters of mufick an Itallian tafte fhould prevaile; but there were other incidents that contributed to eftablifh it; one of the cheif was the coming over of the works of the great Corelli,†

---

* "The younger Matteis," fays Dr. Burney (*Hift. of Muf.* iii. 516, note), "muft have returned to England foon after Mr. North's *Memoirs of Mufic* were written; as I remembered to have feen him at Shrewfbury, where he was fettled as a language mafter as well as performer on the violin, in 1737. I afterwards learned French and the violin of this mafter, who continued at Shrewfbury till his deceafe, about the year 1749. He played Corelli's folos with more fimplicity and elegance than any performer I ever heard."

† Corelli publifhed his firft *Twelve Sonatas* at Rome in 1683. In 1685, thefe were followed by a fecond feries, which appeared under the title of *Balleti da Camera.* In 1690 appeared the third feries, and in 1694, the fourth, which, as they confifted of movements adapted to the dance, he termed, like the fecond fet, *Balleti da Camera.* But his folos, the work by which he acquired the greateft reputation during his lifetime, did not appear till the year 1700, when they were publifhed at Rome, under the following title: *Sonate à Violino, e Vio-*

thofe became the onely mufick relifhed for a long time; and there feemed to be no fatiety of them, nor is the vertue of them yet exhaled; and it is a queftion whether it will ever be fpent; for if mufick can be immortall, Corelli's conforts will be fo. Add to this, that moft of the yong nobillity and gentry that have travelled into Itally affected to learne of Corelli, and brought home with them fuch favour for the Itallian mufick, as hath given it poffeffion of our pernaffus. And the beft utenfill of Apollo, the violin, is fo univerfally

---

line o Cembalo, Opera Quinta, Parte prima, Parte feconda, Preludii, Allemande, Corrente, Gighe, Sarabande, Gavotte, e Follia. Corelli's works appear to have been known in England in 1693, as T. Brown, in a copy of verfes addreffed to Purcell, and prefixed to the fecond book of Henry Playford's *Harmonia Sacra*, publifhed in that year, has the following couplet:

> "In thy productions we with wonder find
> BASSANI's genius to CORELLI's join'd."

The fonatas of this great inftrumental writer were firft circulated in England in MS. In the *London Gazette* for Sept. 23, 1695, (No. 3116,) is the following advertifement. "Twelve Sonatas, (newly come over from Rome,) in 3 parts, compofed by Signeur Archangelo Corelli, and dedicated to his Highnefs the Elector of Bavaria, this prefent year 1695, are to be had fairly prick'd, from the true original, at Mr. Ralph Agutter's, Mufical Inftrument Maker, over againft York Buildings, in the Strand, London." In the *London Gazette*, for July 11, 1700, Mr. Banifter advertifes from his houfe in Brownlow Street, Drury Lane, "The new Sonatas of the famous Sig. Archangelo Corelli, curioufly engraven on 70 Copper-Plates, and printed on a large Imperial paper, being now brought from Rome, will be ready to be delivered to Subfcribers." And in the fame paper, Aug. 29, 1700, Walfh advertifes "Corelli's Twelve Sonatas in Two parts, being his fifth and laft opera. Engraven in a curious character, being much fairer, and more correct in the Mufick than that of Amfterdam." It has been hitherto fuppofed that Walfh did not commence the publication of Corelli's works before 1710.

courted, and fought after to be had of the beft fort, that fome fay England hath difpeopled Itally of viollins. And no wonder after the great mafter made that inftrument fpeak as it were with humane voice, faying to his fcollars—*Non udite lo parlare.* But not fatisfyed with that, the gallants muft have the voices themfelves, fet off in Operas as amply as hath bin knowne in Itally. But how long this humour will hold without back-fliding into Ballad-finging I cannot forfee, tho a fair proffer hath bin made of it in the celebrious and beloved enterteinment of the Beggar's Opera, which made a nightly affembly of the *beau mond* at the Theater for above a month uninterruptedly.*

---

* The *Beggar's Opera* was brought out in the feafon of 1727-8 ; and its popularity was altogether of the higheft clafs. It became at once the fingle fubject of theatres, converfation, books, engravings, and popularity in all its fhapes for an extraordinary length of time. It was played in the provincial theatres with almoft its London frequency, to the thirtieth and fortieth night ; at Bath and Briftol fifty ; it fwept every thing of rivalry from the ftage in Wales, Scotland, and Ireland ; it was performed even in Minorca ; its fongs were the only mufic of the fafhionable world ; its poetry was carried about on fans ; its fcenes and mufic met the eye on fcreens, and all the grotefque and orna-mental furniture of that ftately day, of the toilet and the drawing room. The actrefs whom chance flung into the part of Polly was fuddenly exalted into the poffeffion of every talent under heaven. She was fabricated into even a wit ; and books were publifhed, containing the bon-mots and repartees of Mifs Fenton ! Her picture eclipfed all the noble portraitures of the day ; her " life" was invented and publifhed ; her face and perfon became the ftandard of grace ; her drefs fuperfeded French millinery, and laft and moft improbable of all glories, her fongs drew back the noble worfhippers from the Italian Opera.

The mufic of this celebrated piece confifts of ballad airs (fome of them of great antiquity) to which Gay adapted the words of his fongs. Among them

A large fcene might be opened here to prefent a view of the prefent ftate of mufick in England. But why all that which every body knows, and moft hearers better then myfelf? And what a work would it be to enumerate the mafters regnant, with their caraders, and the number of conforts, fonatas, and concertos, befides folos innumerable, bred and

62.
Conclufion.

are feveral of the fineft Scotch melodies; a circumftance which probably arofe from Gay's refidence in Edinburgh with his patron the Duke of Queenfberry. The airs were provided with accompaniments, and prepared for performance, by Dr. Pepufch.

It has been generally faid that the *Beggar's Opera* was intended to ridicule the Italian Opera; an evident miftake, for there is not the flighteft attempt to burlefque or parody the Italian dramas or mufic, to which it has not the fmalleft refemblance, either in fubjed, ftyle, or form. The fecret of the *Beggar's Opera* is its admirable adaptation to the peculiar turn of the Englifh mind; its found fenfe, its fhrewd fatire on general human nature, its vigorous feizure of national charader, and finally its hits at men in office. For much curious information conneded with the origin and fuccefs of the *Beggar's Opera*, fee the following works: *Memoirs of Macklin; Memoirs of Lee Lewis; Life of Gay; Hogarth's Memoirs of the Mufical Drama; Blackwood's Magazine*, 1826.

The wonderful fuccefs of the *Beggar's Opera* gave rife to a long feries of ballad operas, which have been entirely overlooked by our dramatic and mufical hiftorians. The following is a lift of fome of thefe, printed in odavo with the mufic:—*The Quaker's Opera*, 1728; *Penelope*, 1728; *Love in a Riddle*, 1729; *The Village Opera*, 1729; *Momus turned Fabulift*, 1729; *The Chambermaid*, 1730; *Fafhionable Lady*, 1730; *The Devil to Pay*, 1731; *The Generous Freemafon*, 1731; *The Jovial Crew*, 1731; *Silvia, or the Country Burial*, 1731; *Devil of a Duke*, 1732; *The Lottery*, 1732; *Flora*, 1732; *Achilles*, 1733; *The Boarding School*, 1733; *The Cobler's Opera*, 1733; *The Livery Rake*, 1733; *The Whim*, 1734; *The Plot*, 1735; *Trick for Trick*, 1735; *The Coffee Houfe*, 1737; *The Beggar's Wedding*, 1739; *The Hofpital for Fools*, 1739; *The Intriguing Chamber Maid*, 1750; *The Lover his own Rival*, 1753; *The Mock Dodor*, 1753, &c.

born here, or brought from abroad; the magnificences of the
Operas, the famous organs, organifts, and builders; the various focietys, and affemblys for mufick; efpecially the new
royall Society* (if it continues now as formerly) with many

---

* This eftablifhment, under the title of the Royal Academy of Music,
was the refult of a plan formed by a number of diftinguifhed members of the
ariftocracy for patronifing and carrying on the Italian Opera. A fund of 50,000*l.*
was raifed by fubfcription among the firft perfonages of the kingdom, his Majefty George I. contributing 1000*l.* The fubfcribers were incorporated into a
fociety or company, whofe affairs were conducted by a governor, deputy governor, and twenty directors. The firft year the Duke of Newcaftle was
governor; Lord Bingley, deputy governor; and the directors were the Dukes
of Portland and Queenfberry, the Earls of Burlington, Stair, and Waldegrave,
Lords Chetwynd and Stanhope; Generals Dormer, Wade, and Hunter; Sir
John Vanburgh; Colonels Blathwart and O'Hara, and James Bruce, Thomas
Cole of Norfolk, Conyers D'Arcy, Brian Fairfax, George Harrifon, William
Pulteny, and Francis Whitworth, Efquires. In Dr. Burney's fale (lot 1048)
was " A curious Deed on Vellum with the identical Signatures of the Noble-
men and Gentlemen forming the Original Inftitution of the Corporation of the
Royal Academy of Mufick in 1719." It was purchafed by Bartleman, and
appeared in his fale catalogue (lot 1409). It was afterwards in the poffeffion
of the late William Upcott.

The founders of the Royal Academy proceeded in their enterprife with great
fpirit. Handel, who at that time was refiding with the Duke of Chandos at
Canons, was engaged as compofer, and commiffioned to procure fingers; and
Bononcini and Attilio Ariofti, compofers of reputation on the Continent were
alfo engaged to write operas. Handel immediately proceeded to Drefden, where
Italian operas were then performed with great fplendour at the court of Auguftus
King of Poland and Elector of Saxony; and there he engaged Senefino, Beren-
ftadt, Bofchi, and Signora Duraftanti. Notwithftanding the efforts of three
great compofers, aided by the ftrongeft company of performers that had ever
been affembled in England, the Royal Academy of Mufic did not profper.
About 15,000*l.* of the capital fubfcribed was fpent in the courfe of little more
than a year from the eftablifhment of the academy; and the fubfcribers appear

other varietys, which muficall gentlemen hereafter would be glad to know, if there were a genius apt and fufficient to tranfmitt it to them. But I fhould be very prefumptuous to undertake it, being for many years an alien to the faculty, and at prefent a deprivado : and fhould rejoyce to receive fuch information as I wifh myfelf able to give. And pretending to that is beyond my limits, for what hath Hiftory to doe with the prefent? And if anything of that kind hath already efcaped, it is *ultra crepidam*, and pardon defired.

to have become very reluctant to anfwer the calls made upon them, as appears from the advertifements publifhed by the directors in the newfpapers, urging the payment of the inftalments in arrear, and threatening the defaulters with the " utmoft rigour of the law." A new mode of fubfcription was therefore adopted. Intimation was made to the public, that tickets for the enfuing feafon fhould be iffued on thefe terms : that each fubfcriber, on the delivery of his ticket, fhould pay ten guineas; that, on the 1ft of February enfuing, each fubfcriber fhould pay a further fum of five guineas, and five guineas more on the 1ft of May. The academy promifed fifty performances, and obliged themfelves to allow a deduction proportionably, in cafe they did not give that number. This announcement, which was made on the 25th of November 1721, was the origin of the plan of an annual fubfcription, free from all rifks or demands beyond the amount, which has been followed ever fince.

Notwithftanding the zeal with which its mufical management was conducted by Handel, the feries of beautiful works which he himfelf furnifhed, and the efforts of the firft performers of the age, the affairs of this eftablifhment never profpered, and it clofed its exiftence in 1728, the year in which Roger North's *Memoirs* were written.

FINIS.

INDEX TO THE NOTES.

C. Whittingham, Chiswick.
1846.

For EU product safety concerns, contact us at Calle de José Abascal, 56–1°,
28003 Madrid, Spain or eugpsr@cambridge.org.

www.ingramcontent.com/pod-product-compliance
Ingram Content Group UK Ltd.
Pitfield, Milton Keynes, MK11 3LW, UK
UKHW040620240426
470322UK00010B/225